Shirley Botsford

with DECORATING FABRIC CRAFTS

30 decorating projects from the best-selling author of Daddy's Ties

Shirley Botsford's
DECORATING
with
FABRIC CRAFTS

Published by

Krause Publications
700 East State St., Iola, WI 54990-0001
Telephone (715) 445-2214
www.krause.com

Please call or write for our free catalog of publications. Our toll-free number to place an order or obtain a free catalog is (800) 258-0929 or please use our regular business telephone (715) 445-2214 for editorial comment and further information.

Illustrations and patterns by Shirley Botsford
Photographs by Tony Cenicola unless otherwise credited

Library of Congress Catalog Number: 98-84109

ISBN 0-87341-677-5

Printed in the United States of America

Dedication

This book is dedicated to Jean Denzinger Botsford, my mother, who taught me to sew and showed me how to decorate my first doll house when I was about four years old. Her inspiration has provided me with a creative career in sewing and teaching that I love. Her enthusiasm for decorating has motivated me to continuously design new projects and share my ideas in my books and patterns.

Acknowledgments

*B*efore I even begin writing a book, there is a wonderful group of supportive people that have made it possible for me to pick up a sketch pad or sit down at my lap top! Thank you to all my family, friends, and students for their encouragement.

James Howard Botsford, my Father, the inspiration for my book, *Daddy's Ties* and an inventor whose memory has held my hand through each project and every page.

Gary Botsford, my Brother, who has supported all my ideas, no matter how crazy they seemed, in ways that make it possible for me to keep going...and going.

Charles Fincham, my Friend, without whom I would not have this wonderful house to decorate.

Tony Cenicola, the photographer who shares my enthusiasm and optimistic ability to see all things in their best light.

Pam Hoffman, a friend and partner in thousands of stitchery projects for the last twenty years.

Credit and a big hug goes out to all the makers and motivators who have been involved in the concepts and projects in this book. Their hearts and sometimes their sewing machines have made projects out of what seemed like impossible ideas.

Virginia Avery

Ann Boyce-Kline

Pat Campbell

Dale Conklin

Alex Dupré

Kathy Ettinger

Joan Fincham

Mary Forsell

Donna Fredericks

Janet Jappen

Linda McGehee

Priscilla Miller

Deann Murphy

Asher Pavel

Donna Wilder

Marinda Stewart

Thank you to those who came to my rescue when I needed a special prop, a helping hand, the dishes washed, or just moral support when I was suffering from a bout of "writer's block."

A Corner In Time - Audrey and Stephen Kish
Karen Abramson
Lois Ciesielski
Country Heritage Antiques Center -Richard Triggiani
Early Everything - Gail Boccia
Lorrie Durkin
Ellen Durso
The Family Business - Judith Noorlander
Paul Fincham
The Fincham Family
Norma Hallabaugh
Violet Hoffman

Kringles - Ron Irassi
Lisa Luber
Judy A. Parrey
Kathi Schmitter
Shirley & Henry Stevenson
Maria Sudol
Bobbie Suratt
Karen and Butch Tangen
Stephanie Tangen
Gail Vasquez
Shirley Wersebe
Jennifer Wilmshurst

I am especially grateful to my new friends at Krause Publications, especially my editor Barbara Case, who helped me turn my ideas into a reality as seen here in this beautiful book. My thanks too, to Jan Wojtech, who did such a spectacular job on the layout and design.

My superheroes are the people and the companies that make all the tools and materials that go into turning my designs into projects.

A special thank you goes to Pfaff Sewing Machines of America for such wonderful machines and answers to my endless questions.

Bucilla
Clotilde Inc., Clothilde
Coats & Clark, Meta Hoge
Conso Products
Creative Beginnings, Debi Linker
Distlefink Designs, Deann Murphy
Fairfield Processing Corp., Donna Wilder
Freudenberg Nonwovens/Pellon, Tina Schwager
Ghee's, Linda McGehee
Hi-Fashion Fabrics
JHB International

Lace Country, Patty Katz
Offray Ribbon, Ellie Schneider
Olfa Products Group
Omnigrid Inc.
Pfaff American Sales Corp.
Prym-Dritz, Dianne Giancola
Rosebar Textiles
S & S Appliance Inc., Bunny and Stuart Davis
Simplicity Pattern Co.
Sulky of America
Walnut Hollow Farm
Wm. E Wrights Co.

Foreword

I remember being introduced to Shirley Botsford through the craft and decorating pages of national magazines like *Family Circle, Woman's Day,* and *Good Housekeeping,* with the same byline, "Designed by Shirley Botsford." Her quilting, stitchery, sewing, and home decorating projects were so varied and so eye-catching, I decided, as a craft manufacturer, to look her up. Shirley and I met and soon discovered that we were both working on the art of braiding, a classic craft that was long overdue for a design update. We combined her creative and my manufacturing forces to produce a complete line of braiding fabric, tools, and books. Shirley's designs included everything from small accessories like baskets and picture frames to accent rugs that you could coordinate to your own interiors. Her fabric colorations and ingenious braided home dec projects were an instant hit. Fabric crafters were delighted with the simple tools, easy instructions, and simplified techniques. Under Shirley's artistic eye, small scraps of fabric were turned into a quilter's palette that became braided heirlooms.

Shirley would make presentations at trade shows, always dragging along what we referred to as her "magic trunk." A trade show is a bit like a circus - you start with a plain floor and ugly pegboard walls to display your merchandise. We couldn't wait for Shirley to arrive to "create" our booth. Out of her trunk would come bolts of fabric and plain walls became transformed with shirring, pleating, and bows. We'd all stand ready with irons and staple guns as she would provide the vision. I'll never forget the time she opened her trunk and unrolled an entire Victorian house facade, all appliquéd using her latest designer line of fabrics. It was complete with windows, flower boxes, gingerbread, and even a front door. Front porch rockers with cushions and oval braided rugs emerged from the trunk too. Needless to say, the booth was a show stopper.

At these industry events, Shirley's workshops and classes were always standing room only. She presented tips and ideas for beginners as well as the most sophisticated store owners. Nothing daunted her, if the glue gun or iron broke, if the braiding tools had been damaged in transit, if materials had not arrived - Shirley made each event a creative experience in the same way that she turned scraps into heirlooms.

Using this same ingenuity, I watched Shirley transform her hilltop Victorian home overlooking the Hudson River from a handyman's nightmare into a bed and breakfast, where needleworkers flock for classes and inspiration. Every nook, displaying her decorative needlework, makes participants want to learn more. This new book, *Decorating with Fabric Crafts,* will surely inspire and encourage you to make wonderful things for your own home.

Deann Murphy

Introduction

I am writing this book for homemakers everywhere. Especially those who surround themselves with things that they make themselves. It is for stitchers and home decorators of every description, beginning with the first cave dweller who celebrated their natural decorating instincts by drawing on their walls for reasons that may have had nothing to do with function. It celebrates the spirit of creativity in all of us. It is a project book for the decorator at heart, inspired by a wonderful house that decorated itself.

Shirley Botsford

Photos by Frank Riemer for Fairfield Processing Corp.

I frequently express what's going on in my life by working things out with some sort of stitching project. This four-piece garment, done for the 1996-97 Fairfield Fashion Show, entitled "Botsford Briar" is a perfect example. This ensemble reflects my new lifestyle in the 1889 Queen Anne Victorian home I am transforming into a retreat for quilters and stitchers. Both this outfit and the Botsford Briar Bed & Breakfast fulfill my lifelong dream of living in my own dollhouse. High on a hill, my plum-colored Victorian house address is number 19, as I have appliquéd on the front of the quilted bag. The full-length crushed velvet skirt is embellished with entwined bias taffeta vines with golden thorns cut from metallic rick-rack and inserted with machine embroidery. An old-fashioned trellis in the rose garden was the inspiration for the jacket. The center front panel has lace lattice that supports hundreds of ribbon and fabric roses of every description. The flared jacket is quilted with the feather stitch to reflect the rose vines. The camisole with lace sleeves features an appliquéd fabric portrait of the house on the front, creating a one-shouldered design using the distinctive round three-story turret of the house.

Contents

Chapter One

THE HOUSE THAT DECORATED ITSELF

Set high on a hill, originally built by a hat maker so he could see his factory across the Hudson River, this 1889 Queen Anne Victorian is 5,800 square feet of pure Victoriana. It has some breathtaking views sprinkled with marinas and passing ships all along the river. It serves as a location for photographers, small weddings, and magazine articles and was featured in the movie "Nobody's Fool" starring Paul Newman and Melanie Griffith. Shirley's studio is on the third floor, with the design room in the top of the turret. Stitching retreats frequently take over the whole house and its five bedrooms. Individual classes and workshops are given in one of the large bedrooms on the second floor. The first floor has a tea room, spacious parlor, formal dining room, sun room, large foyer, kitchen, and a wonderful old-fashioned pantry. The character of this house is defined by ornate carved details, paneled doors, and original woodwork with a beautiful staircase and four decorative fireplaces, all of which have provided the inspiration for the projects in this book.

EARLY ARCHITECTURAL INFLUENCES

Observe Everything Around You

I grew up in a colonial style house, quite unaware of architecture in general. The house had some wonderful woodwork, hardwood floors, and glorious hardware details. It was terribly efficient and cozy, but never really "spoke" to me. I think that those simple surroundings are the basis for my Victorian cravings. I definitely had developed an early appreciation for classic architectural details, but I was not prepared for the effect that seeing my very first Victorian would have on me. I guess I was about ten, and on taking a new route in my walk to school, I turned the corner onto a different street and was confronted with my first gingerbread-covered Victorian house. It stopped me in my tracks and I was consumed by the sight of this full-size doll house. I whispered a promise to myself right then and there, "Someday I'm going to live in a fancy house just like that."

> *"You can never go home again."*
> *- Thomas Wolfe*

MAKING CHANGES

Do Things Differently

After spending 16 years in New York City running my own design business, it was time to escape. Like lots of other people, the hustle and bustle of the city had taken its toll and I needed to revive my creativity with a new environment. As a textile designer working for big companies, I did lots of traveling to manufacturing plants to check the colors and designs as the fabrics were being printed. One of my favorite trips was to a small textile mill in the Hudson River Valley, several hours north of New York City. I would rent a car and drive north through what I fondly call the "long green tunnel." The road winds along the Hudson River, giving you endless scenic views of water, mountains, and trees, trees, trees! The destination was a small, river town filled with streets full of Victorian houses. I remember thinking that if I ever left New York City, this is the type of place where I would want to be.

> *"A woman's life is like a great house with many different rooms. Some doorknobs remain unturned."*
> *- Edith Wharton*

When I finally decided to leave the city, I once again drove that long green tunnel north, looking for someplace large and wonderful that I could afford. I remembered that little town full of Victorians and headed there like a refugee, full of hope. The town had changed a lot and most of the neighborhoods full of those houses that I remembered had been demolished for a new highway. Having almost given up, as I continued to drive through town, I spotted a row of Victorian houses on a hill near the river. Its distinctive character was visible from the highway and I headed right for it. It felt like a step back in time to around the turn of the century. The house at the top of the hill looked just right and after about three months of selling everything I had, I found a way to make it mine. After signing the final papers, I said to myself, "Keeping promises to yourself makes you feel like you're ten years old again!"

CREATING HOME SWEET HOME

Celebrate What You Have

Photo by Roger Craig Merritt

The original kitchen in the house was in the cellar. It must have been a wonderful old brick oven with a large hearth area for cooking. This kitchen on the first floor was the original serving or warming kitchen. High ceilings and tall windows welcome everyone to breakfast. The wainscoating is a light shade of plum similar to the outside of the house.

When the day came to move into my own Victorian house, I was in store for a real adventure. I expected to have lots to do, but I never imagined the overwhelming task that was ahead. After setting up a temporary kitchen, I headed to the real heart of the house - the sewing room. I had always wanted a room for my sewing machine and this big old house gave me a choice. I picked the room with a high ceiling and a beautiful old window with the best southern exposure. I had to start setting things up right away because I was working on an article and had a quilt due in a week. Putting the sewing machine in front of the window is always a good idea for me since I spend so much time working and the light keeps me going. As I shoved it into place, I glanced out the window and really noticed the view for the first time. Framed in my sewing room window was the Victorian house next door. It reminded me of the house I had seen as a child. A large round three-story turret is topped off with a pointed slate roof. A stained glass window, three "gingerbread" porches, wonderful architectural details, and beyond that a view of the Hudson River. Challenged like never before, I admitted, "It takes a lot of work to make dreams come true and a comfortable spot with a great view is a good place to start."

"In solitude we give passionate attention to our lives, to our memories, to the details around us."
- Virginia Woolf

WELCOME TO THE HOUSE THAT DECORATED ITSELF

Look for Opportunities

My sewing machine faced the Victorian house next door for a little over eight years. Every day, while I was working, I looked out the window and enjoyed seeing the house in different seasons and times of the day or night. Light falling on the decorative architectural details created intricate shadows and produced constantly changing color effects. Gradually I fell in love with that house and wished that I could be sewing over there. The opportunity to make it mine came suddenly, without any notice. Seemingly beyond my reach, I committed to pursuing one obstacle after another just in case there was any hope of success.

After what seemed like an endless process that lasted almost a year, the house key was in my hand. Thirty minutes after signing the final papers and writing checks for amounts that I thought were definitely beyond my means, I put my house key on a big red tassel and headed for home. As I slipped the key into the lock, I remember thinking, "This house is going to take very good care of me."

> *"Style has nothing to do with money. Anybody can do it with money. The true art is to do it on a shoestring."*
> *- Tom Hogan*

Photo by Roger Craig Merritt

A perfect place to escape from the rest of the world, this nostalgic sun room is really the original back porch that was converted by adding 14 windows some time during the 1920s when a major modernization added real bathrooms to the house. It's a natural spot for vintage wicker, handmade quilts, and patchwork pillows created from old fabrics recycled from men's ties.

The front parlor is directly off the main foyer and was probably used as a reception area and ladies tea room. Separated by enormous, beautifully paneled pocket doors from the larger gentleman's parlor, it is sunny and bright. With almost floor to ceiling windows, it is located directly off the expansive front porch, making it the first room everyone sees. A fireplace with an oak mantle and mirror accented by a crystal chandelier make guests feel like they have stepped back in time.

"Have nothing in your homes that you do not know to be useful and believe to be beautiful."
- William Morris

MOTIVATING FACTORS

Take Some Risks

With a big, empty house on your hands, the first thing you think of is curtains. Armed with pencils, tape measure, yardstick, and a small notebook, I marched into the house to find out what curtains would be needed. Faced with my first window, I quickly realized that I needed to go out and buy an eight foot ladder. Why hadn't this occurred to me before I bought the house? The sudden realization that I might be saying this about a lot of things flashed through my mind. Remaining undiscouraged, I unloaded the ladder from the top of my car and maneuvered it into the front parlor. After measuring a few windows, I experienced another temporary setback. I needed a much bigger notebook. Maybe it would be a good idea to count the windows so I knew just how big a notebook it should be. Out of breath on the third floor, I found that I had to say it out loud a few times just to get used to the fact that I was the proud owner of a house with 79 windows.

Being short on funds, I decided that I would put up just lace curtains. Well, you can do the math, 79 times whatever the curtains would cost, and they were all very big windows. Perhaps I need a home equity loan. Desperate but still feeling pretty positive, I decided to make the curtains myself and save money. Luckily, a friend of mine had a lace company and I called her immediately. We laughed about making curtains for 79 windows and made a deal for her discontinued patterns. After calculating yardages for days, I ordered and shifted into high gear to address the next challenge - curtain rods! Whenever my friends would comment on my situation, I would just say, "I'm not in charge anymore, the house wants this."

SOURCES OF INSPIRATION

Discover Something You Love

Having exhausted my savings by purchasing the house and putting up the curtains, I knew I would have to do without anything else for quite some time. My first instinct was to fill the house up with furniture, but that was not an option. Nothing, however, was going to spoil my enthusiasm. The sewing room was going on the third floor and I would concentrate on that first so I could get back to work as soon as possible.

> "A house is who you are, not who you ought to be."
> - Jill Robinson

Photo by Roger Craig Merritt

The Victorians always gave the best room in the house to their guests and this is it. It's called "The Magnolia Room" and if you stayed here, it would certainly be your favorite room. Facing south and west towards the Hudson River, this spacious bedroom has its own balcony with a fabulous view that is actually an old-fashioned sleeping porch where breakfast is served on warm mornings.

After hundreds of trips, carrying studio supplies down the stairs next door, across the lawn and up two flights... I was in! When I was done, I looked out my window from the top of the turret and noticed that I had actually worn a bare path in the lawn from all the trips.

I scattered my plants throughout the first and second floors. I got quite used to not having much furniture in the rest of the house. I began to notice all the wonderful architectural details. I think that if the house had been full of furniture, this would not have happened. Whenever I feel like I've run out of ideas, I boost myself up by saying, "Creative problem-solving is, more often than not, good design."

Old bathrooms are always a real challenge to decorate. This one is the "water closet" as shown on the original blueprints for the house. Having gone through only a few modern changes, it retains its original claw foot tub and unusual wainscoating. My decorating secret is to start with a rug you love. Using all the colors in the rug, conceive a decorating scheme. I used the coordinated shades in the rug for towels and accessories. An antique spool chest is the perfect size for extra linens and sundries.

TRANSFORMATIONS

Turn Ideas Into Projects

After a year or so, I started to add more furniture. I just couldn't resist auctions and yard sales. Having studied the architecture for such a long time, picking out the right furniture was easy. Bringing home each piece and setting it down in the perfect spot was so rewarding. Soon the house was filled up, but something was missing. I needed pillows and quilts and all those soft accessories that make a house feel like home. Realizing that I was facing another enormous project, I looked around for some ideas. I found it right there in the house. Sitting on the sun porch (which I call my inspiration room), I tried to sketch things to make for the different rooms. Somehow nothing seemed right. I was looking for a theme or something to relate to the house. The idea suddenly came to me that the design ideas were all around me. The architectural details that were now so familiar to me would provide all the inspiration I needed for the projects. I spent the next few days racing around the house, making sketches, photographing the architectural details, and planning the final stage of my decorating project. As I have said many times in my lectures, "Find something that you really love, allow it to take over and you'll do beautiful things."

Photo by Roger Craig Merritt

Shirley has given flower names to all the bedrooms in the house. This bright sunny room with a southern exposure, originally the master bedroom, is called "The Rose Room." Eastlake style furniture creates a romantic vintage setting accented with quilts and pillows made from antique fabrics.

"There has never been a house so bad that it couldn't be made over into something worthwhile."
- Elsie de Wolfe

GETTING STARTED

See Things In a New Way

Accessories are usually added to an interior setting without much thought. This often creates chaos and clutter. Sometimes living with lots of "stuff" projects an unorganized and eclectic message. The idea is to enhance what you have rather than starting over. When you simplify the setting and focus on carefully designed things that reflect and blend with the environment, everything is improved. You can surround yourself with things that you love making and create your own personal decorating style. Throw out all the rules and put together a plan based on your own possessions. Create a more personal environment that showcases your work.

For example, let's say you want to make a special table setting for a family reunion. Start early and begin by selecting a holiday or special occasion as your target date. This gives you a time frame and deadline to work with. This motivates you to get going and actually finish the project.

First, try to imagine the table setting you want to create. Get your dishes out and serving platters and any of your favorite things. Set the table, then omit things that seem out of place. Get a color scheme going based on what you have. Remember, anything that you add has to complement what you already have. Perhaps you decide to make place mats. Closely examine the items you have selected, looking for a color scheme and a motif you can use. Trust yourself, you can do this!

Using tracing paper held over the dishes, draw some of the motifs that you like. Go to your fabric stash and collect anything that might work. Back at the table, spread the fabrics around and eliminate anything that you don't like. Select colors for the place mats and appliqué motifs. Make a rough sketch of the place mat design, placing the appliqués where they look best. Try a few options and ask friends for their opinions. Take your final drawings to the copy center and have them enlarged to the size that would look good. Clear up any rough lines and unevenness. Make patterns and templates for the place mats from the copies. Try these out on the table with the dishes, to check size and design placement. Select the fabrics you want to use and make one place mat. Check it with the dishes and then you're ready to make the rest. When you are finished, if you have time, think about adding napkins and other accessories using the same design. Add pieces gradually until you have a whole table full of accessories coordinated to your own dishes. This is how I designed all the things in this book, working with the architectural details and what I had. Try it yourself and I think you will be pleased with the results!

Chapter Two

THE SCALLOP AND THE BUTTON

V eneers and decorative moldings surround hand-painted panels for no purpose at all other than embellishment. This is a language that I clearly understand and have chosen to celebrate in the pages of this book. At the top of my list is something I fondly refer to as the scallop and the button. Already two of my favorite motifs in my sewing endeavors, the scallop and the button have provided me with an appetite for accessorizing in new ways.

Tea Time Again

*T*his Teapot Cozy and its coordinated table linens are a marriage of the scallop and button motif and the violets on my favorite teapot. This chapter shows you how to make a four-piece set of tea accessories that are sure to charm visitors.

TEAPOT COZY

Finished Size:
12" high x 16" wide

WHAT YOU'LL NEED:

- linen fabric:
  - ⅜ yard ivory
  - ½ yard lavender
- ⅝ yard violet-print fabric
- ½ yard fleece
- ½ yard paper-backed appliqué fusible
- 14 brass buttons ⅝" size
- gold metallic thread

PIECES TO CUT:

FIND THE PATTERNS IN THE PULL-OUT INSERT

- ivory linen - 2 Teapot Cozy #1
- lavender linen - 2 Teapot Cozy Handle #2; 2 Teapot Cozy Spout #3;
  2"-wide bias strips to equal 28"
- appliqué fusible - trace 2 upper and 2 lower appliqué sections to the paper side; roughly cut a rectangle around each section
- violet print - 2 Teapot Cozy #1 for lining; fuse the appliqué sections to the wrong side and cut out on lines following the manufacturer's instructions
- fleece - 2 Teapot Cozy #1; 2 Teapot Cozy Handle #2; 2 Teapot Cozy Spout #3

HOW TO MAKE IT:

1. Using Teapot Cozy #1 as a placement guide, remove the paper and fuse the violet-print appliqué sections to the right side of both ivory linen pieces.

2. Baste fleece to the wrong side of each cozy, handle, and spout piece.

3. With right sides together, stitch the two curved sides of the handle pieces together. Trim, turn right-side-out, and press flat. Stitch trim and turn the spout in the same way, leaving the insertion edge open.

4. Quilt the cozy front and back using Teapot Cozy #1 as a guide. Satin stitch the raw edges of the appliqué sections with metallic thread. Stitch a button to the point of each scallop.

5. Cut a 4" length of lavender bias. Fold in half, match and stitch the 4" edges. Trim, turn right-side-out, press, and form a loop by basting the raw ends together.

6. Match the raw edges and baste the loop, handle, and spout to the cozy front.

7. With right sides together, stitch the cozy front and back together. Assemble the violet-print lining in the same way. Turn the cozy right-side-out and insert the lining inside so wrong sides are together. Baste the bottom edges together.

8. Seam the bias pieces together as needed. Bind the bottom edge with lavender bias. Hand tack the lining to the top edge inside so it stays up inside.

Project BORDERED NAPKIN

Finished Size: 16" x 16"

WHAT YOU'LL NEED:

- ½ yard ivory linen fabric
- ½ yard violet-print fabric
- ½ yard paper-backed appliqué fusible
- 2 brass buttons ⅝ " size
- gold metallic thread

PIECES TO CUT:

FIND THE PATTERNS IN THE PULL-OUT INSERT

- ivory linen - 1 Bordered Napkin #4
- appliqué fusible - trace the appliqué border to the paper side and cut out
- violet print - place the border on the wrong side of the fabric; fuse and cut on the lines, following the manufacturer's instructions

HOW TO MAKE IT:

1. Using Bordered Napkin #4 as a guide, remove the paper and pin the violet-print border to the right side of the ivory linen. Working flat, fuse one section at a time.

2. Satin stitch the inner raw edges of the appliqué border with metallic thread. Stitch a button to the point of each scallop.

3. Make a ¼" narrow double hem around the entire outer edge of the napkin, mitering the corners for a neat finish.

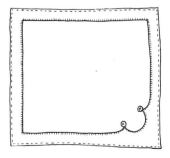

Shirley Suggests

*When working with paper-backed appliqué fusible, it is best to draw the design on the paper side and cut it out roughly ¼" **outside** the lines. Then fuse it to the wrong side of the appliqué fabric. Then cut directly on the design lines. This way, the fabric and paper are cut simultaneously. This produces a well-fused edge and a more accurate appliqué design.*

Project MUFFIN WARMER

Finished Size: 20" x 20"

WHAT YOU'LL NEED:

- linen fabric:
  - ¾ yard ivory
  - 1 yard lavender
- ½ yard violet-print fabric
- ¾ yard flannel
- ¾ yard paper-backed appliqué fusible
- 16 brass buttons ⅝ " size
- gold metallic thread

PIECES TO CUT:
FIND THE PATTERN IN THE PULL-OUT INSERT

- ivory linen - 1 Muffin Warmer #5
- lavender linen - 2"-wide bias strip to equal 86"
- appliqué fusible - trace the appliqué border to the paper side and cut 2 halves
- violet-print fabric - 1 Muffin Warmer #5 for lining; place the halves of the appliqué border together on the wrong side so they form a complete border; fuse and cut out on the lines, following the manufacturer's instructions
- flannel - 1 Muffin Warmer #5

HOW TO MAKE IT:

1. Using Muffin Warmer #5 as a placement guide, remove the paper and pin the violet-print border to the right side of the ivory linen. Working flat, fuse one section at a time.

2. Baste the flannel to the wrong side of the linen.

3. Satin stitch the inner raw edges of the appliqué border with metallic thread. Stitch a button to the point of each scallop.

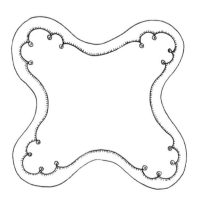

4. With wrong sides together, baste the violet-print lining to the muffin warmer.

5. Seam the bias pieces together as needed. Bind the entire outer edge with lavender bias.

Shirley Suggests

For a fine finish, seam the ends of the binding together with a diagonal seam. This eliminates bumps caused by multiple layers of fabric overlapping in one spot.

Project OVAL TRAY MAT

Finished Size: 17" x 26"

WHAT YOU'LL NEED:

- ½ yard ivory linen fabric
- ½ yard violet-print fabric
- ½ yard fleece
- ¾ yard paper-backed appliqué fusible
- 6 yards 1½"-wide lavender taffeta ribbon (or 2 yards pleated trim)
- 16 brass buttons ⅝" size
- gold metallic thread
- pleater board (to make your own trim)

PIECES TO CUT:

FIND THE PATTERN IN THE PULL-OUT INSERT

- ivory linen - 1 Oval Mat #6
- appliqué fusible - trace the appliqué border to the paper side and cut 2 halves
- violet-print fabric - 1 Oval Mat #6 for lining; place the halves of the appliqué border together on the wrong side so they form a complete border; fuse and cut out on the lines, following the manufacturer's instructions
- fleece - 1 Oval Mat #6

HOW TO MAKE IT:

1. Using Oval Mat #6 as a placement guide, remove the paper and pin the violet-print border to the right side of the ivory linen. Working flat, fuse one section at a time.

2. Baste the fleece to the wrong side of the linen.

3. Quilt the mat using Oval Mat #6 as a guide. Satin stitch the inner edges of the appliqué border with metallic thread. Stitch a button to the point of each scallop.

4. Following the manufacturer's directions, use a pleater board to create ¼" pleated ribbon trim to equal 66".

Shirley Suggests

The amount of trim produced by different pleaters will vary. Make a small test on your pleater to determine how much ribbon you will need - generally three to four times the finished length. Carefully seam ribbon ends or extra lengths as needed on the inside of a pleat so it is not visible from the front.

5. Stitch one edge of the pleated ribbon trim around the oval mat edge, placing right sides together.

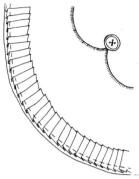

6. Pin the lining on top, right sides together. Stitch around the entire outside edge, leaving a 6" opening for turning. Trim, turn, and press. Slipstitch the opening closed.

Chapter Three

FROM THE HEARTH

*A*s I was struggling for a theme around which to create a decorating book, my eyes fell on the tiles of one of the fireplace hearths in my home. The similarity between tiles and patchwork momentarily flashed through my mind. I realized that I had looked at this hundreds of times, frequently up close, but had never made this connection before. I suddenly realized that the theme for my book was all around me. I spent the next few hours rushing from room to room "seeing" the architectural details of my home in a new way for the first time.

Fireside Memories

A simple tile design gives life to a piecework pattern that uses ribbons to make special projects meant for a precious few. This chapter includes heirloom projects suitable for gift giving when you're looking for a teddy bear, decorated box, or a photo album.

SENTIMENTAL SEWING BOX

Finished Size: 10" x 10" x 5" high

WHAT YOU'LL NEED:

- 10" round box with lid to cover
- ribbon:
    - 1½ yards 1¼"-wide red velvet ribbon
    - 3¼ yards 1"-wide burgundy woven ribbon
    - 1½ yards ⅜"-wide black/gold woven ribbon
    - 5¼ yards 1½"-wide black/gold woven ribbon
- ⅜ yard fleece
- 10" x 10" piece black felt
- 2 yards ⅛" black/gold twisted cord
- ½" gold ball button
- gold metallic thread
- white glue
- gold paint

PIECES TO CUT:

- ribbon - cut 1½ yards from all ribbons except the 1½"-wide black/gold woven
- fleece and felt - using the box bottom as a pattern, cut one circle from each

HOW TO MAKE IT:

1. Paint the inside of the box and lid gold.

2. Using metallic thread and a wide satin stitch, stitch the entire length of ⅜"-wide black/gold woven ribbon to the 1"-wide burgundy woven ribbon. Butt the edges of the ribbon together as you feed them under the presser foot. Center the satin stitches over the edges of the two ribbons. Repeat, adding the 1¼"-wide red velvet ribbon next to the burgundy woven ribbon.

Shirley Suggests

Using a tear-away stabilizer under the satin stitching will keep it flat and eliminate any tension problems. Cut 1"-wide strips from the stabilizer and insert them under the butted edges of the ribbon as you stitch. Tear them away as you complete each row.

3. Press the three combined ribbons. Using a ruler with a 45° angle, cut the ribbon strip in a zigzag manner so you have triangles of pieced ribbon.

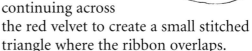

4. Arrange four triangles in a square with the red velvet at the center point. With right sides together, baste two triangles together, matching the satin stitched seams. Join the two other triangles in the same way. Join the two pairs of triangles in a square and press.

5. Mark the center of the fleece circle by folding it in quarters. Working flat, baste the pieced ribbon square to the center of the fleece circle.

6. From the remaining triangles, make four pairs, placing the red velvet at the base of the triangle. Baste one to each side of the center square, butting the edges together. Corners will overlap at the center of each side. Satin stitch the butted edges, continuing across the red velvet to create a small stitched triangle where the ribbon overlaps.

7. Satin stitch lengths of the remaining ribbons to the outer edges of the ribbon square until the ribbon extends evenly ½" beyond the fleece circle. Stitch the button in the center.

8. Glue the ribbon top to the box lid. Glue the ½" allowance down to the side of the lid, clipping so it will lay flat. Glue the burgundy ribbon over the edge of the lid, turning under the raw ends where they meet.

9. Glue cord to the upper and lower edges of the lid. To neatly finish the end of the cord, dip it in white glue and allow it to dry thoroughly, trim it off sharply, and butt the ends together where they meet.

10. Measure the height of the box side and add 1". Cut lengths of the 1½"-wide black/gold woven ribbon. Satin stitch them together on the long edges into one piece to fit around the box sides.

11. Glue the joined ribbon to the box side, centering it so ½" extends at the top and bottom edges. Tuck under any excess and trim as needed.

12. Fold and glue the ½" extensions at the bottom and top edges of the box, clipping as needed. Glue a piece of ribbon over the raw ends on the inside of the box. Glue the felt circle to the bottom.

KEEPSAKE RIBBON BEAR

Finished Size: 18" tall (standing)

WHAT YOU'LL NEED:

- ribbon:
  2 yards each: 2¼"-wide black velvet, ivory moiré, gold metallic, burgundy satin, and woven ribbon 1¼ yards 2"-wide red wired-edge ribbon
- ½ yard flannel
- ¼ yard gold metallic fabric
- large bag stuffing
- 2 eyes
- button for nose
- red and black felt scraps
- gold metallic thread
- 4 teddy bear joint sets

PIECES TO CUT:

FIND THE PATTERNS IN THE PULL-OUT INSERT

- ribbon - cut all ribbons in 18" lengths
- gold metallic - 2 Teddy Paw #7; 2 Teddy Sole #8
- flannel - 2 pieces 18" x 22 "; 2 Teddy Paw #7; 2 Teddy Sole #8
- red felt - 1 Teddy Tongue #14
- black felt - 2 Teddy Eyelash #15

HOW TO MAKE IT:

1. Beginning at the 18" edge on one of the pieces of flannel, baste one burgundy satin ribbon strip to the flannel. Baste the other ribbons next to it in the following order - ivory, woven, gold, and black. Continue until the flannel is completely covered. Repeat this on the other flannel piece.

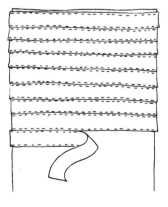

2. Using metallic thread and a wide satin stitch, stitch the butted edges of the ribbon together. Center the satin stitches over the edges of the two ribbons. Repeat this for all the ribbon edges. Press flat.

3. With right sides together, pin and baste the two ribbon sections together. Match the ribbons on the two layers. Lay out Teddy pattern pieces #9, #10, #11, #12, and #13, following the ribbon guidelines. Make a second paper pattern for the arms, legs, and ears because you need two pairs of each. Check to make sure that the pieces are cut in symmetrical pairs so the ribbons will match at the seams.

4. With right sides together, pin the curved outer edges of the Teddy Ear #9 together. Match the ribbon seamlines. Stitch using a small straight stitch. Trim, turn, and press. Match the straight raw edges and gather them up to 3". Repeat to make the second ear. Baste the ears to the front body pieces as indicated by the dots.

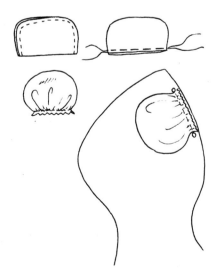

5. Back the paw pieces with flannel and quilt on the lines. Appliqué the paw pieces to the lower arm along the line, making one left and one right. With right sides together, pin two arm pieces together. Match the ribbon seamlines. Stitch with a small straight stitch, leaving an opening to stuff between the dots. Trim, turn, and press. Repeat for the other arm.

6. Back the soles with flannel and quilt on the lines. Stitch the two leg pieces together as you did the arms. Leave the straight edges at the foot open. With right sides together, pin and stitch the soles to the straight open edges of the leg, matching the dots to the seams. Turn right side out. Repeat to make the second leg.

7. Make the darts on the back body pieces. Stitch the center back seam, leaving an opening to stuff.

8. Stitch the center front seam on the front body. Back the eyes with the black felt eyelashes and stitch or glue them in place. Attach the nose and tongue.

9. Stitch the front and back body pieces together. Install the arm and leg joints, following the manufacturer's instructions.

10. Stuff the arms, legs, and body. Slipstitch all the openings closed. Tie the bow at the neck.

Stitch and flip the quilted paw pieces in position on each inner arm piece, making a pair.

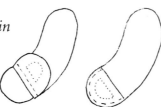

Stitch the inner and outer arm pieces together, leaving an opening for turning.

Quilt the soles and stitch the leg pieces together, leaving an opening for turning. Do not stitch the sole edges.

Stitch the sole to the bottom of the leg. Turn right side out through the opening.

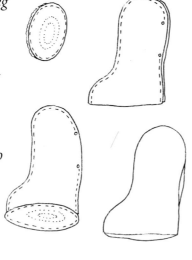

Shirley Suggests

To add weight and make the bear sit up better, use polyester stuffing pellets mixed with regular stuffing in the legs and lower body.

MEMORIES FAMILY ALBUM

Finished Size: 13" x 15" high

WHAT YOU'LL NEED:

- 13" x 15" scrapbook to cover
- ½ yard black velvet
- ribbon:
    1 yard ½"-wide copper metallic ribbon
    1 yard 2½"-wide black moiré ribbon
    1 yard 1½"-wide woven ribbon
- 1 yard ¾"-wide gold filigree trim
- 1¾ yards ⅛" black/gold twisted cord
- 1 small brass label frame
- 2 gold tassels
- 2 copper beads with ⅛" holes
- gold metallic thread
- 2 sheets heavy decorative paper 13" x 15"
- white glue

PIECES TO CUT:

- black velvet - 2 pieces 16" x 18"

HOW TO MAKE IT:

1. Remove the front and back cover of the scrapbook. Lay the velvet out flat with the wrong side up. Mark the position of the cover on the velvet so 1½" extends evenly beyond all sides. Use a brush to apply a thin coat of glue to the outside front cover and place it on the wrong side of the velvet as marked. Repeat this with the back cover. Check to make sure the velvet is smooth.

2. Fold the excess fabric to the inside covers, mitering the corners and gluing it in place. Trim off the excess fabric.

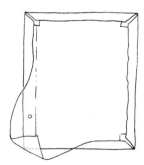

3. Using metallic thread and a wide satin stitch, stitch the entire lengths of ribbon together side-by-side in the following order - black moiré, copper metallic, and woven. Stitch the gold filigree trim to the outer edge of the woven ribbon.

4. Cut a 18" strip of the combined ribbons. Glue this to the album cover front, placing it so about ½" of the black moiré ribbon can be folded to the inside at the left edge. Glue all the ribbon edges to the inside of the front cover.

5. Fold the combined ribbon strip to make a triangle over the upper right corner of the album front. Measure along each side to make sure they are the same. Glue it in place, trimming off the excess on the inside. Repeat this on the lower right corner.

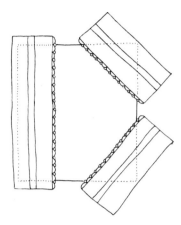

6. Cut the decorative paper to fit the inside covers. Glue it in place so all raw edges are concealed.

7. Make a personal label and glue it inside the brass frame centered on the velvet, about 10" up from the bottom edge.

8. Use a knitting needle to punch the holes for the ties through the velvet and ribbon. Re-assemble the album and insert the twisted cord through the holes as it was originally done. Use the plastic eyelets if your scrapbook has them.

9. Slip a bead on each tie end and put the end back through the bead, forming a loop. Hand stitch the tassel to the loop. Put a dot of white glue inside the bead and pull the loop through so the tassel and cord are glued to the bead. Trim off the free end of the cord.

Chapter Four

CARVING OUT
A GREAT WELCOME

As you arrive at my house, one of the first things most people notice is the wood carvings. Having no woodworking skills to relate to, the first thing I see is fabric and ribbons. After looking closely at the details, I immediately wanted to transform every surface into stitches. By doing this, I was giving back the colors and the textures that surely inspired this original labor of love in the first place.

Reasons to Celebrate

*T*he wood carver's art is captured in fabrics and ribbons for fanciful decorative elements that are a feast for the eye. The table runner, topiary, and bell pull make elegant appointments to a formal dining room. Although they represent the carving that inspired them almost identically, each one seems to take on a character quite unlike the versions in wood.

Project GOLD LEAF APPLIQUÉ RUNNER

Finished Size: 30" x 60"

WHAT YOU'LL NEED:

- 1¾ yards burgundy "crinkled" taffeta
- burgundy taffeta:
    1¾ yards for backing
    1⅝ yards for making the pleated trim (or buy 4¼ yards purchased pleated trim or fringe)
- 1¾ yards gold lamé
- 3¼ yards paper-backed appliqué fusible
- 1½ yards fleece
- 4¼ yards 1/8" burgundy/gold twisted cord
- gold metallic thread
- pleater board (to make your own trim)

PIECES TO CUT:

FIND THE PATTERNS IN THE PULL-OUT INSERT

- crinkled taffeta - 1 Table Runner #16
- appliqué fusible - trace the appliqué sections to the paper side, making 2 lefts and 2 rights; roughly cut a rectangle around each section
- gold lamé - fuse the appliqué sections to the wrong side and cut out on the lines, following the manufacturer's instructions.
- fleece - 1 Table Runner #16
- plain taffeta - 7"-wide strips to equal 4¼ yards

HOW TO MAKE IT:

1. Using Table Runner #16 as a placement guide, remove the paper and pin one appliqué section to the right side of the crinkled taffeta. It's best to fuse one quarter of the design at a time.

Don't cut the appliqués out until you are ready to fuse them down because they tend to curl up and become tangled. Note that the appliqué sections have a curlicue at the center that overlaps the center line so they appear interlocked when appliquéd.

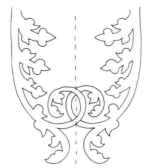

2. Baste the fleece to the wrong side of the runner.

3. Machine satin stitch all the raw edges of the appliqué design with metallic thread.

4. Following the manufacturer's directions, use a pleater board to create ¼" pleated trim from fabric. Cut 7"-wide fabric strips and seam them together using a bias seam to make long pieces for pleating. To avoid hemming the pleats, simply fold the fabric in half before pleating it so the fold becomes the "hem" edge.

5. Stitch the raw edges of the pleated trim around the runner edge.

6. With right sides together, pin the lining on top and stitch around the entire outside edge, leaving a 10" opening for turning. Trim, turn, press, and slipstitch the opening closed.

7. Couch cording around the edge of the runner. Place it in the ditch between the runner and the pleating. Use invisible thread and a wide machine zigzag stitch to couch it in place. Stabilize the ends of the cord with fabric glue or seam sealant and butt them together.

Project

Finished Size: 6" x 36"

RIBBON
EMBROIDERY
BELL PULL

WHAT YOU'LL NEED:

- 1⅛ yards mauve moiré
- ¼ yard fleece
- ¼ yard heavy interfacing
- 2¼ yards ¼" brown/gold twisted cord
- large gold tassel
- 6"-wide bell pull bracket

PIECES TO CUT:
FIND THE PATTERN IN THE PULL-OUT INSERT

- moiré - 1 piece 11" x 34" for embroidery; 1 Bell Pull #17 for backing
- fleece and interfacing - 1 Bell Pull #17 of each

HOW TO MAKE IT:

1. Mark the center of one of the 11" x 34" moiré pieces. Transfer the design to the center on the right side of the moiré, using Bell Pull #17 as a placement guide. Baste the interfacing to the wrong side, positioning it under the bell pull outline.

2. The design is embroidered using only three stitches. The satin stitch is used for most of the design. Use the stem stitch for stems and outlining. French knots add texture at the top of the flower.

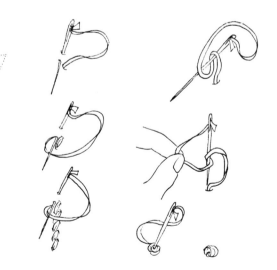

Satin Stitch   Stem Stitch   French Knot

Shirley Suggests

Try my "butt & zig" method for doing quick couching by machine. Use invisible thread and a very narrow zigzag stitch. Butt the cord up against the finished edge of the project and place it under the presser foot. Stitch so that one side of the stitching catches the edge of the cord and the other secures it to a few threads of the project. Adjust the stitch width so the zigzag stitching virtually disappears into the "ditch" between the project and the cord.

3. The subtle color variations have been achieved by using variegated hand-dyed silk ribbons. Using the photo as a guide, work the colors as follows:

leaves - shades of green
stems - medium brown
grapes - shades of purple
flower - shades of gold and
        yellow
flower center - purple and
        fuchsia
French knots/flower outline -
        lavender
flower base - green

4. Using the placement guide, center the completed embroidery and cut out the bell pull shape. Baste the fleece to the wrong side. With right sides together, stitch the side and bottom edges of the bell pull. Trim, turn right side out through the top, and press.

5. Beginning at the top edge, apply the cording to the side and bottom edges. Couch the cording around the edge, easing extra in at the corners.

6. Hand sew the tassel to the bottom part of the bell pull behind the cording.

7. Finish the top end by pressing the raw edges to the inside and slipstitching them flat. Insert the top end through the bell pull bracket and hand tack securely.

Project

Finished Size: 16" x 26" high

HANDMADE LILY TOPIARY

WHAT YOU'LL NEED:

- 1½ yards each of 1½"- to 2½"-wide wired-edge ribbon in the following colors: three shades of purple, peach, gold, ivory, rose, burgundy, pink
- 8 to 12 dried hydrangeas
- flower centers
- stem wire
- green floral tape
- 24 gauge floral wire
- 25 to 30 leaves
- large container
- Styrofoam cone tree base 24" tall

PIECES TO CUT:

- cut 10 lengths of each of the 9 ribbon colors as follows:

6"-lengths to make 18 small lilies (total 90 lengths)
7"-lengths to make 18 medium lilies (total 90 lengths)
8"-lengths to make 18 large lilies (total 90 lengths)

HOW TO MAKE IT:

1. Plan your topiary so you have equal numbers of small, medium, and large lilies in each color. For this large topiary, you will be making 54 lilies.

2. Fold one piece of ribbon in half, forming the point of the petal. Using a tweezers, grasp the wire end on one side of the ribbon. Push the ribbon along the wire, gathering it up evenly to the fold. Repeat on the other side.

3. Twist the wire ends together and gather in the free edges of the ribbon, forming a petal with the gathered edges together at the center. Twist the wire around the base of the petal to secure. Pinch the end of the petal to make a point. Make five petals for each lily.

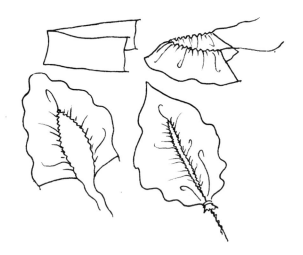

4. Arrange five petals to make a flower. Insert a flower center in the middle and secure with wire to a 4" to 5" piece of stem wire. Wrap the wire tightly around the base of the lily to hold all the parts together. Cover the ribbon ends of the flower base and the stem wire with floral tape. Make six flowers in each color.

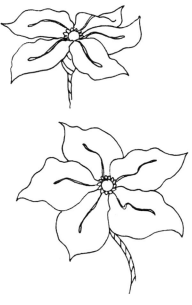

5. Divide the dried hydrangeas into sections about the size of an orange. Insert them into the Styrofoam base, spacing them evenly about 3" apart. If the stems are not strong enough, use stem wire and floral tape to create clusters of hydrangea blossoms as you did for the lilies.

6. Insert the ribbon lilies between the hydrangeas, distributing the colors and sizes evenly. Arrange the lilies so they completely cover the base. Make about 24 clusters of leaves using stem wire and floral tape. Scatter them evenly around the topiary, inserting them between the lilies and hydrangeas.

Shirley Suggests

Spray the completed topiary lightly with a clear acrylic spray. This stabilizes the dried hydrangea petals a bit and makes the topiary easier to keep clean.

Chapter Five

MANTEL OF LEAVES

I find that those who sew often have a green thumb, or at least a green finger or two hiding out beneath their thimbles. I am no exception. I consistently seek out plants to nurture and have even been caught watering thirsty ones in office buildings and restaurants. The leaves on this mantle are doing just fine on their own, but when my mother gave me her china, I chose to welcome it to my home amidst some leafy accessories.

Every Day Is Special

This classic leaf design and my mother's blue china have joined forces to create a simple but beautiful table that will welcome you to breakfast on a daily basis. Treat yourself by using it every day to start each morning off right.

CENTERPIECE/ BISCUIT BASKET

Finished Size: 8" x 12" x 5" high

WHAT YOU'LL NEED:

- ¼ yard light blue print fabric
- ½ yard dark blue print fabric
- ¼ yard fleece
- 8" x 12" piece navy felt
- ⅛ yard paper-backed appliqué fusible
- 8" x 12" x 5" oval box to cover
- ⅝" cover button
- medium blue thread
- white glue

PIECES TO CUT:
FIND THE PATTERN IN THE PULL-OUT INSERT

- light blue print - cut a piece to fit your container, adding 1" to all outer edges
- appliqué fusible - trace the Centerpiece Basket Appliqué #18 on the paper side; roughly cut a rectangle around the design
- dark blue print - 3 braiding strips 3"-wide to equal 30"; fuse the appliqué to the wrong side and cut out on the lines, following the manufacturer's instructions
- fleece - cut a piece to fit the container sides exactly
- felt - cut an oval, using the box bottom as a pattern

HOW TO MAKE IT:

1. Using Centerpiece Basket Appliqué #18 as a placement guide, remove the paper and fuse the dark blue appliqué to the right side of the light blue piece.

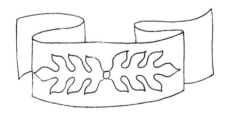

2. Satin stitch the raw edges of the appliqué with medium blue thread. Cover the button in dark blue fabric and stitch it to the center of the appliqué.

3. Apply a thin coat of white glue to the sides of the container and cover with fleece. Pin the appliquéd piece over the fleece. Allow 1" to extend beyond the box at the top and bottom edges, making sure the appliqué is straight on the front. Turn under 1" at the center back seam and glue.

4. Fold and glue the extra fabric to the bottom and inside of the box, clipping as needed. Glue the felt oval to the bottom.

5. Fold under the raw edges on three fabric strips. Hand tack them together and braid for a length of 9". Cut the strips, leaving 1" ends. Repeat this to make a second handle. Shape the braid into a handle and space the ends 2" apart. Glue the ends of each braided handle to the inside of the container, spreading them out flat.

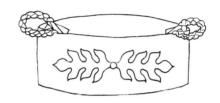

Shirley Suggests

If you plan to use the container open, for biscuits etc., line the inside with fabric. Glue a piece of ribbon around the top inside edge to finish it off neatly. To decorate both sides, place an appliqué on each side of the container, positioning the seam at one side.

Project QUILTED PLACE MAT & NAPKIN

QUILTED PLACE MAT

Finished Size: 12" x 19" wide

WHAT YOU'LL NEED:
(to make one place mat)

- ⅜ yard light blue print fabric
- ⅛ yard dark blue print fabric
- ¼ yard white eyelet fabric
- ½ yard fleece
- ¼ yard paper-backed appliqué fusible
- 1 yard ⅝"-wide eyelet trim
- medium blue thread

PIECES TO CUT:
FIND THE PATTERN IN THE PULL-OUT INSERT

- light blue print - 2 Place Mat Appliqué #19; 1 piece 12½" x 18½" for place mat back
- appliqué fusible - trace the place mat appliqué on the paper side twice; roughly cut a rectangle around each one
- dark blue print - fuse the appliqués to the wrong side and cut out the lines, following the manufacturer's instructions
- 9" x 12½" piece of white eyelet for place mat center
- 12½" x 18½" piece of fleece

HOW TO MAKE IT:

1. Using Place Mat Appliqué #19 as a guide, remove the paper and fuse one appliqué to each light blue side panel.

2. With right sides together, stitch one appliqué side panel to each side of the eyelet center. Press the seams towards the sides.

3. Baste the fleece to the wrong side of the place mat front.

4. Satin stitch the raw edges of the appliqué with medium blue thread.

5. Cut two 13" pieces of eyelet. Hem each raw end by turning over ¼" twice. With right sides together, baste one to each side of the place mat front.

6. With right sides together, pin the place mat front and back together. The eyelet trim should be caught in the stitching at only the sides of the place mat. Make sure it is not caught in the seam at the top and bottom edges. Stitch around the entire outside edge, leaving a 6" opening at one side for turning. Trim, turn, and press. Slipstitch the opening closed.

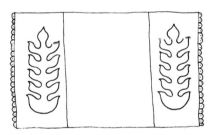

7. Quilt in the ditch of the place mat panel seams.

Shirley Suggests

Make the place mat reversible by using a different fabric (like tiny checks) on the back. Then simply quilt around both leaf appliqué motifs to create quilted borders through to the other side.

APPLIQUÉ NAPKIN

Finished Size: 18" x 18"

WHAT YOU'LL NEED:

- ½ yard light blue print fabric
- ⅛ yard dark blue print fabric
- 2 yards ⅝"-wide eyelet trim
- ⅛ yard paper-backed appliqué fusible
- medium blue thread

PIECES TO CUT:
FIND THE PATTERN IN THE PULL-OUT INSERT

• light blue print - 1 piece 17" x 17"
• appliqué fusible - trace Napkin Appliqué #20 on the paper side and roughly cut it out around the design
• dark blue print - fuse the appliqué to the wrong side and cut out on the lines, following the manufacturer's instructions

HOW TO MAKE IT:

1. Using Napkin Appliqué #20, remove the paper. Crease one corner of the napkin by folding it diagonally in half. Pin the appliqué to the right side on the corner of the napkin about 1" from each edge. Center it on the crease line and fuse it in place. Satin stitch the raw edges of the appliqué with medium blue thread.

2. Stitch a ¼" narrow double hem around the entire outer edge of the napkin, mitering corners for a neat finish. Pin the eyelet trim to the wrong side of the napkin, easing in extra fullness at the corners. Stitch the ends together where they meet. Edgestitch the eyelet trim around the napkin hem.

Shirley Suggests

For a quick edge finish, serge the top of the eyelet trim to the right side of the napkin raw edge. Miter the eyelet by folding it at the corners. Press the seam allowance to the wrong side and topstitch flat.

EMBELLISHED CHAIR COVER

Finished Size: 12" x 20" high, plus ruffles

WHAT YOU'LL NEED:

- ½ yard light blue print fabric
- 1¼ yards dark blue print fabric
- ½ yard fleece
- 1½ yards 2"-wide pleated eyelet trim
- 1½ yards navy piping
- 12" x 20" x 1"-thick foam insert
- medium blue thread

PIECES TO CUT:
FIND THE PATTERN IN THE PULL-OUT INSERT

Note: Measure your chair and adjust the size and yardages as needed.

- light blue print - cut 2 back pieces to fit your chair, adding ½" on all sides; round the top edge using Chair Cushion Appliqué #21 as a guide
- appliqué fusible - trace Chair Cushion Appliqué #21 on the paper side; roughly cut a rectangle around the design
- dark blue print - cut 8 chair ties 4½" x 24"; fuse the appliqué to the wrong side and cut out on the lines, following the manufacturer's instructions
- fleece and foam - cut 1 from each, using the light blue chair back as a pattern

HOW TO MAKE IT:

1. Crease one of the chair back pieces by folding it in half vertically. Working flat, remove the paper, center the appliqué on the crease line, and fuse it in place.

2. Baste the fleece to the wrong side of the appliquéd chair back front.

3. Satin stitch the raw edges of the appliqué with medium blue thread.

4. Baste piping to the raw edges around the chair back front, finishing the end neatly at the bottom corners. Baste the pleated eyelet trim over the piping. Hem the ends.

5. With right sides together, fold one of the tie pieces in half lengthwise. Trim off one end at a 45° angle. Stitch the raw edges together, leaving the straight end open. Trim, turn, and press flat. Baste the raw ends together and form a pleat so the end of the tie is about 1½" wide. Repeat to make a total of eight ties. Baste the ends of two ties to each corner of

the chair back, checking placement on your chair. Pin the ends to the center of the appliqué so they don't get caught in the stitching.

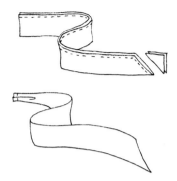

6. With right sides together, pin the back to the front. Use a zipper foot to stitch close to the trim and piping. Leave the entire bottom open. Trim, turn, and press. Cut the foam to fit, insert it, and slipstitch the opening closed.

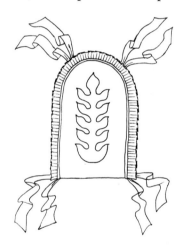

Shirley Suggests

To finish the chair, make or purchase a coordinated, plain seat cover. Appliqué doesn't wear well on the seat, so put all your energy into embellishing the backs and find the easiest solution for covering the seat. Choose the seat first so you can coordinate the back fabrics with it.

Chapter Six

NEWEL POST PLANTINGS

*B*ounding down the stairs at my house you are confronted several times by twin newel posts standing guard, wearing their own garden logos. I like to think of them as miniature ecology posters paying homage to all things flora and fauna. Deciding to spread this subtle message throughout the house by way of appliqué projects has become a personal mission.

Garden Splendor

A natural combination of leaves and buds grows outward from a perfectly round center. Without any color to go by, I used my creative license to "paint" each section with fabrics. This chapter beckons you to return to nature by making a folding screen with stained glass qualities, a quilted over-sized pillow, and a lacy tablecloth in snowy shades of white and ivory.

APPLIQUÉ
PANEL SCREEN

Finished Size: 3-panel folding screen 36" x 70"

What You'll Need:

- folding screen with 15 "photo frame" sections
Note: Measure the frame openings in your screen and adjust the size of the appliqué sections if necessary
- sheer, crisp organdy or firm curtain fabric:
  ½ yard each rose, peach, and green
  1 yard tan
- 1¼" yards 3"-wide gold metallic ribbon
- 3 yards paper-backed appliqué fusible
- 2 yards translucent, heavy fusible craft interfacing
- 4 spools gold metallic thread

Pieces to Cut:
Find the patterns in the pull-out insert

- fusible interfacing - 15 base pieces 8½" x 10½"
- appliqué fusible - trace Appliqué Panel Screen #23, #24, #25, #26, #27, and #28 on the paper side; group them together according to the color fabric they are to be cut from; space them ⅛" apart to fit on the fabric yardage and fuse the entire piece to the wrong side of the fabric before cutting them out; follow the manufacturer's instructions
- rose sheer - 30 Appliqué Panel Screen #23; 30 Appliqué Panel Screen #25
- peach sheer - 30 Appliqué Panel Screen #24; 30 Appliqué Panel Screen #26
- green sheer - 60 Appliqué Panel Screen #27
- tan sheer - 15 pieces 8½" x 10½" for backgrounds
- gold ribbon - 15 Appliqué Panel Screen #27

Shirley Suggests

Make one practice appliqué section to test the heat tolerance of your fabrics. Adjust the iron temperature so the fusible will work without shrinking or distorting the appliqué shapes.

Shirley Suggests

Be sure to protect your iron and board from fusible by using scrap fabric or paper as a pressing cloth. Since you are working with sheer fabrics, a good amount of fusible is going to seep through the fabric.

How to Make It:

1. Fuse one interfacing piece to the wrong side of each tan background. This stabilizes the base for the appliqué work and gives them a translucent quality much like stained glass.

2. Pin one tan base piece over the Appliqué Panel Screen Placement/Stitch Guide #22. Remove the paper from the appliqué pieces one at a time and fuse them in place in numerical order.

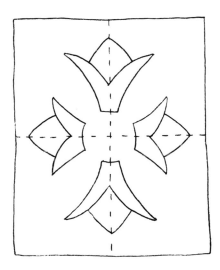

Notice the ⅛" overlaps in some areas. These will be covered by satin stitching. Trace the design lines in the leaves on the appliqué. Repeat to make 15 panels.

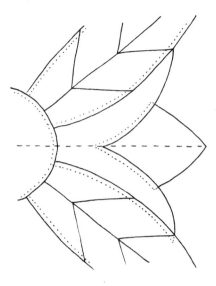

3. Satin stitch the raw edges and design lines with metallic thread. Follow the stitching sequence shown for a fast, neat, continuous stitching method that minimizes finishing thread ends. Stitch the lines in the following order - dotted lines, solid lines, dashed lines. Next stitch the two sides of the four leaves. Finish by stitching the center circle.

4. Press and trim the outer edges to fit the "photo frames" of your folding screen. Insert the finished appliqué sections between the glass according to the manufacturer's directions as you would a photo.

QUILTED PORCH PILLOW

Finished Size: 28" x 28"

What You'll Need:

- 26" square pillow form
- ⅝ yard lavender moiré
- 1½ yards green brocade
- ⅛ yard hunter green damask
- ¼ yard mauve satin
- ¼ yard purple taffeta
- 1½ yards fleece
- 3 yards ⅝"-wide purple piping
- ¾ yard paper-backed appliqué fusible
- 8 purple tassels
- 22" green zipper
- green variegated metallic thread

Pieces to Cut:
Find the patterns in the pull-out insert

- green brocade - 2 pillow backs 27½" x 27½"; 4 borders 4" x 27½"
- lavender moiré - 1 background 20½" x 20½"
- appliqué fusible - trace Quilted Porch Pillow Appliqué #29, #30, #31, and #32 on the paper side; draw 4 of each, grouping them together by color; roughly cut them out; fuse the appliqué pieces to the wrong side of the fabric and cut out on the lines, following the manufacturer's instructions
- mauve satin - 4 Quilted Porch Pillow Appliqué #29
- purple taffeta - 4 Quilted Porch Pillow Appliqué #30
- hunter green damask - 4 Quilted Porch Pillow Appliqué #31
- green brocade center - 1 Quilted Porch Pillow Appliqué #32

How to Make It:

1. Fold the lavender moiré background in quarters, crease, and open it out flat. Remove the paper and pin the appliqué pieces in place using Quilted Porch Pillow Placement/Stitch Guide #33 as a guide. Butt the edges of the appliqué pieces against each other and fuse in place.

2. Stitch the green brocade borders to the outer edges of the lavender moiré. Miter the corners and trim off the excess fabric. Baste the fleece to the wrong side of the pillow front. Use a decorative stitch to quilt in the ditch of the border seams.

3. Transfer the design lines to the leaves. Satin stitch the raw edges and design lines with metallic thread. Add three rows of decorative stitching and quilting in the buds and use double rows in other areas as desired for extra embellishment.

4. Baste piping to the raw edges around the pillow front, finishing the ends neatly at the center of one side.

5. Insert the zipper in the 27½" seam of the two pillow backs. With right sides together, pin the back to the front. Use a zipper foot to stitch close to the piping. Trim, turn, and press.

6. Hand stitch two tassels to each corner of the pillow behind the piping.

LACE COLLAGE TABLECLOTH

Finished Size: 52" x 52", plus fringe

What You'll Need:

- lace fabric:
  - ⅝ yard white
  - ⅜ yard ivory
  - ⅜ yard cream
  - 1½ yards tan
- lace trim:
  - 4⅝ yards ⅝"-wide ivory flat
  - 2⅛ yards ¾"-wide white flat
  - 2⅜ yards 1"-wide tan gathered
- 2⅜ yards ⅜"-wide cream flat ribbon trim
- 6 yards 4"-wide gold fringe
- 11" diameter crocheted doily

Pieces to Cut:

Find the patterns in the pull-out insert

- tan lace - 53½" x 53½"
- appliqué fusible - trace Lace Collage Tablecloth Appliqué #34, #35, and #36 on the paper side; draw 4 of each, grouping them together by color; roughly cut them out; fuse the appliqué pieces to the wrong side of the lace and cut them out, following the manufacturer's instructions
- ivory lace - 4 Lace Collage Tablecloth Appliqué #34
- cream lace - 4 Lace Collage Tablecloth Appliqué #35
- white lace - 4 Lace Collage Tablecloth Appliqué #36

How to Make It:

1. Fold the tan lace piece in quarters, mark the folds with pins, and open it out flat. Remove the paper and pin the appliqué pieces in place on the center of the tan lace. Use the photo as a guide. Butt the edges of the appliqués against each other and fuse in place.

2. Cover the raw edges of the appliqués with trims as indicated below. Finish the trim ends by overlapping them or tucking under ¼". All raw edges at the center are covered by the crocheted doily. Stitch it down after all the trims are in place.

> ¾" white lace - outer edges of buds
> 1" tan gathered lace - inner V-shaped areas of petals
> ⅜" cream ribbon - topstitch over raw edges of gathered lace on petals
> ⅝" ivory lace - two long sides of leaves

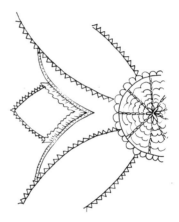

3. Press under ¼" hem on the tablecloth edges. Stitch the fringe to the outer edges using two rows of topstitching.

Chapter Seven

FRETWORK FANCIES

W hen confronted with my first gingerbread-encrusted Victorian house at about the age of ten, I vowed to someday live in one of my own. Much to my delight, there is a sprinkling of this fancy filigree not only on the outside of my home, but inside too. This wonderful wheel and fan combination is the crowning glory of the staircase. Borrowing the designs for a bed full of pillows is a great way to enjoy this fretwork up close.

Lace Enchantment

When interpreting architectural details into a needle art technique, it's essential to consider all the possibilities. This design went through more changes than any other in the book and I almost eliminated it. It's important to keep trying every option because there is an ideal technique waiting to showcase every design. I find that the designs that give me the biggest challenge are the ones that turn out the best.

QUILTED BUTTON SHAM

Finished Size: 17" x 26", plus ruffles

WHAT YOU'LL NEED:

- 17" x 26" pillow insert
- ⅝ yard peach velveteen
- ⅜ yard ivory satin
- ½ yard pink moiré
- 1 yard paper-backed appliqué fusible
- 1½ yards ⅜"-wide pink ribbon
- 2½ yards ¾"-wide lace trim
- 1 yard ¾"-wide scalloped braid trim
- 2½ yards 2½"-wide gathered double lace ruffle trim
- 2½ yards ⅜"-wide ivory decorative cord
- 9 pearl buttons 1"-size
- 22" peach zipper
- pink thread

PIECES TO CUT:

- peach velveteen - 17½" x 26½" background; 2 pillow backs 10" x 26½"
- appliqué fusible - draw 10" circle and 13" circle and roughly cut them out
- pink moiré - fuse the 13" circle to the wrong side and cut out on the lines, following the manufacturer's instructions
- ivory satin - fuse and cut out the 10" circle as you did for the pink moiré

HOW TO MAKE IT:

1. Fold the peach background in quarters, mark the folds with pins, and open it out flat. Fold both circles in quarters and crease the fold lines, marking the quarters.

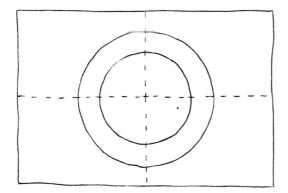

2. Remove the paper and fuse the moiré circle in the center of the sham, matching the quarter marks. Repeat, fusing the ivory satin circle to the center of the moiré circle. Use Quilted Button Sham Center #37 as a guide. Baste the fleece to the wrong side of the sham front.

3. Divide the ivory circle into eighths and draw placement lines for the ribbon using Quilted Button Sham Center #37 as a guide. Edgestitch the pink ribbon across the circle diameter, over the lines. Overlap each piece at the center. Place the cut ends of the ribbon at the edge of the ivory satin.

4. Using Quilted Button Sham Center #37 as a guide, quilt a triangle-shaped wedge in each segment of the circle. Stitch a button in the center and at the halfway point on each ribbon spoke.

Shirley Suggests

Make a pretty round pillow by using just the two appliqué circles. Use the large circle as a pattern for the pillow front and back. Insert a lace ruffle and cording as for the sham.

---

5. Topstitch the scalloped braid around the inner edge of the ivory circle, using it to conceal all the raw edges. Butt the straight edges of the lace trim next to it and topstitch it around the circle. To finish, turn under ¼" on the ends of the braid and lace trims. Repeat this with the lace trim on the outer edge of the moiré circle.

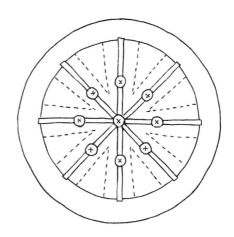

6. Beginning at the center and working outward, draw a 2" grid on the peach background. Quilt the grid lines.

7. Baste the lace ruffle trim to the raw edge around the entire sham front, finishing the ends by turning under ¼".

8. Insert the zipper in the 26½" seam of the two pillow backs. With right sides together, stitch the back to the front. Trim, turn, and press. Couch the cording in the ditch next to the lace ruffle around the entire edge of the pillow. Finish the ends by butting and hand stitching them down.

CUT-OUT FAN PILLOWS

Finished Size: 17" x 17"

What You'll Need:

- ½ yard peach velveteen
- ⅛ yard ivory satin
- ¼ yard pink moiré
- ¼ yard ¾"-wide lace trim
- ¼ yard ¾"-wide scalloped braid trim
- 1¾ yards 2½"-wide gathered double lace ruffle trim
- ½ yard fleece
- ½ yard paper-backed appliqué fusible
- 1¾ yards ⅜"-wide ivory decorative cord
- pink thread
- stuffing

Pieces to Cut:
Find the patterns in the pull-out insert

- peach velveteen - 2 Fan Pillow #40
- appliqué fusible - trace 5 Fan Pillow Appliqué #38 on the paper side; space them 1/8" apart and cut them out as one piece; trace 1 Fan Pillow Center #39 and roughly cut it out
- *Note:* If you are making a pair of pillows, reverse the wavy appliqués to make a mirror image for the second pillow.
- ivory satin - fuse the wavy appliqués pieces to the wrong side and cut the 5 pieces out on the lines, following the manufacturer's instructions
- pink moiré - fuse the fan center to the wrong side and cut out as you did for the ivory satin
- fleece - 2 Fan Pillow #40

How to Make It:

1. Using the Fan Pillow #40 as a placement guide, remove the paper and fuse the wavy appliqués to the peach velveteen. Repeat, fusing the fan center in position.

 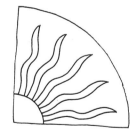

2. Baste the fleece to the wrong side of the velveteen pillow front. Satin stitch the raw edges of the wavy appliqués with pink thread.

3. Topstitch the scalloped braid around the inside edge of the fan center, concealing the raw edge. Butt the straight edge of the lace trim next to it and topstitch it around the outer edge. Make three rows of quilting in the fan center.

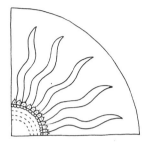

4. Baste the lace ruffle trim to the raw edge around the entire fan pillow front, finishing the ends by turning them under ¼".

5. With right sides together, stitch the back to the front. Leave a 6" opening to turn on one straight side. Trim, turn, and press. Stuff the pillow and slipstitch the opening closed. Couch the cording in the ditch next to the lace ruffle around the entire pillow front, finishing the ends by butting and hand stitching them down.

Shirley Suggests

Use the fan pillow pattern to make a circular table topper. Just combine four fans at the centers and appliqué them to the center of a purchased tablecloth.

ORNAMENTAL MEDALLIONS

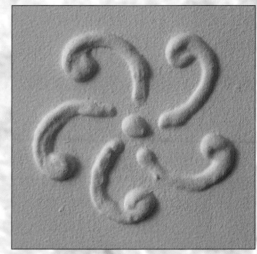

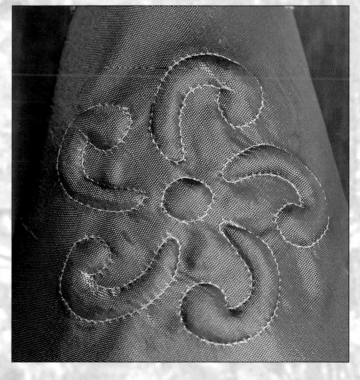

*S*wirling ornamental plaster work dances around the ceiling on the first floor. Small motifs are scattered over the walls like stars in the sky. A former resident recently told me that this technique had once decorated every room in the house. By capturing the essence of the patterns in a new medium, I could spread its decorative qualities everywhere.

Timeless Treasures

The decorated boxes and trapunto lampshade are a direct interpretation of the plaster medallions that decorate the hallway. Brass charms have been substituted on the boxes for a stylized version. The "stitch and stuff" technique used for the lampshade is called trapunto and almost matches the plaster motif exactly.

SKIRTED
JEWELRY BOX

Finished Size: 7" x 7" x 3½" high

TRAPUNTO LAMPSHADE

Finished Size: 7" high with a circumference of approx. 16"

WHAT YOU'LL NEED:

- small lampshade to cover - approx. 7" high

Note: Measure your lampshade and adjust yardages to fit

- ¼ yard blue/green iridescent taffeta
- ¼ yard straight braid edge trim
- ⅝ yard scalloped braid edge trim
- 1 yard ½"-wide gimp trim
- stuffing
- gold beads:

Note: numbers will vary with different trims. Place trim around shade base and count places to attach beads.

    small round beads
    medium round beads
    teardrop beads

- gold metallic thread

PIECES TO CUT:
FIND THE PATTERNS IN THE PULL-OUT INSERT

- blue/green taffeta and muslin - make a pattern for your shade (see below); add ¾" to all sides; cut one each from taffeta and muslin

HOW TO MAKE IT:

1. Since each shade is different, you will need to make your own pattern to fit. Tape pieces of newspaper together to make a sheet large enough for your shade cover. Tape the straight edge of the newspaper to the seam on the shade. Working flat on a table, roll the shade so the paper wraps smoothly around the shade. When you reach the seam where you started, trim off the paper evenly with the seam and tape it in place. Next trim the excess paper from around the top and bottom edges of the shade. Remove the paper from the shade and smooth out any roughly cut edges. Pin the lampshade shape on muslin and add ¾″ turn-under allowance to all edges. Cut this from muslin and then taffeta.

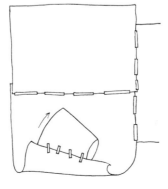
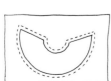

2. Baste the muslin to the wrong side of the taffeta shade cover. Pin this over your lampshade and mark the placement for the Trapunto Lampshade Medallion #41.

3. Working flat, transfer the medallion design to the muslin side. Separate the taffeta and muslin. Using small scissors, make a ¼" long slit in the center of each trapunto area. Make sure you are cutting only the muslin. Put the two layers back together.

4. Baste the two layers together around the entire medallion design. Wind your bobbin with metallic thread and stitch the design lines using a small straight stitch. Pull the thread ends through to the muslin side and knot.

5. Using a knitting needle, carefully insert tiny amounts of stuffing in each stitched area through the slashes in the muslin. Coax the stuffing evenly into all the trapunto areas. Don't stuff too firmly as that will cause puckering. Hand whipstitch the slashes closed.

6. Wrap the shade cover around the shade and pin it in place. Adjust it so an even amount of extra fabric extends at the top and bottom edges. Turn under ½" fabric at the back seam and trim off any excess. Hand stitch or glue the seam in place.

7. Fold the excess fabric to the inside of the shade at the top and bottom edges. Clip it to fit around any wire frame areas inside. Glue the raw edge flat to the inside. To cover, glue the gimp trim over the raw edges.

8. Glue the straight braid trim around the top edge of the shade, overlapping ends ¼" at the back seam. Repeat with the scallop braid trim around the bottom of the shade.

9. Hand sew the beads to the scallop trim with beading thread. Take a stitch through the lower edge of the trim. Insert the teardrop, medium round, and small round beads on the thread. Next, skipping the hole in the small bead, return through the bead

holes, to the trim edge. The small bead becomes the "stop." Secure the thread with a double knot and a drop of glue. Repeat at all the scallops around the bottom edge.

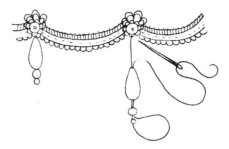

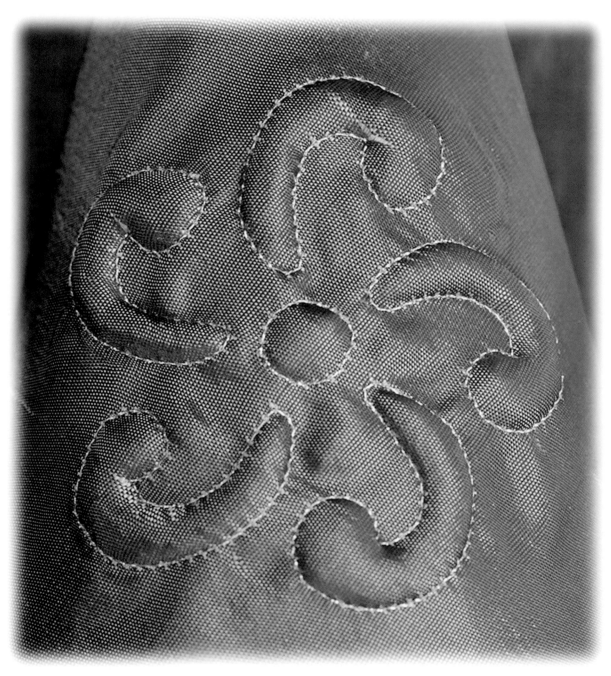

STAINED GLASS VARIATIONS

*I*lluminating the second floor landing is this majestic but rather plain stained glass window. I used to wish it was a much more spectacular pictorial Tiffany window, but I have come to appreciate the daily contribution its plainness makes. It seems that almost every time I pass by, I am redesigning that window. New colors... exciting motifs... my imagination seems to be fed by its pure simplicity.

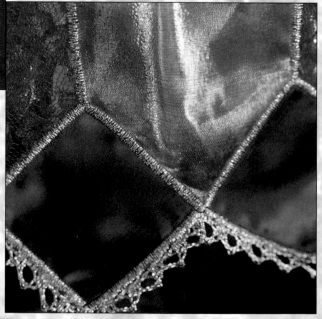

Room With a View

The straight lines of this somewhat simple window design inspired elaborate uses for basic shapes. Adding excitement with the use of texture and color creates a lampshade, pillows, and a doll's dress. Fabric choices of silk and sheers maintain the quality of light and sparkle usually associated with stained glass.

Project

WINDOWPANE PILLOWS

Finished Size: 20" x 20"

WHAT YOU'LL NEED:

(to make one pillow)
- ½ yard red print fabric
- ¼ yard red silk
- ¾ yard gold lamé
- ⅛ yard each of red and purple velvet
- ½ yard fleece
- 2⅛ yards 1"-diameter cotton cord
- gold metallic thread
- 18" square pillow form

PIECES TO CUT:

- red silk - 3 pieces 4" x 18"
- red print fabric - 2 pieces 4" x 18"; 2 pillow backs 10" x 18"
- purple velvet - 6 pieces 2½" x 2½"
- red velvet - 4 pieces 2½" x 2½"
- gold lamé - 4 yards 4"-wide bias strips
- 18" x 18" piece of fleece

HOW TO MAKE IT:

1. Lay the pillow front strips out, alternating the two fabrics. Begin and end with the red silk. Seam them together and press seams open.

2. Position the velvet squares on point, centered at the ends of the strips. Use the photo as a guide. Alternate colors, placing them ½" in from the edge of the pillow front. Baste them in place.

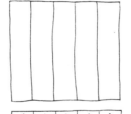
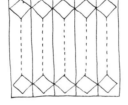

Shirley Suggests

To control slippery velvets that tend to unravel easily, use paper-backed appliqué fusible. Cut 2½" squares and fuse them to the wrong side of the velvet before cutting out the fabric. Cut, remove the paper, and fuse them down on the pillow front.

3. Baste the fleece to the wrong side of the pillow front. Embellish the seamlines with a machine embroidery stitch in metallic thread.

4. Using metallic thread, satin stitch the raw edges of the velvet squares. Begin at one side of the pillow front and stitch one edge continuously in a large zigzag manner across the entire pillow front. Pivot at the corners of the squares. Turn around and stitch back, covering the remaining edges. Repeat at the other end of the pillow front.

5. Draw a line in the center of each fabric strip that connects the corners of the velvet squares. Use a decorative machine embroidery stitch to quilt on these lines.

6. Machine gather both edges of the gold lamé. Pull the gathers up to equal the length of cotton filler cord. With right sides out, fold the gathered lamé over the cord and baste the raw edges together. Baste the cord to the pillow front, turning under the edges of the lamé and trimming the cord to fit.

7. Insert the zipper in the 18" seam on the pillow back. With right sides together, pin the back to the front. Use a zipper foot to stitch close to the caterpillar cord. Trim, turn, and press.

Shirley Suggests

This "caterpillar cord" is one of my favorite edge treatments for pillows. It looks great, but adds a lot of extra time to the finishing. If you prefer, simply use purchased jumbo piping or fringe in a coordinating color.

Project

SHEERLY ELEGANT SHADE COVER

Finished Size: 16" high with 36" circumference

What You'll Need:

- lampshade to cover (cover will fit a round shade up to 30" in circumference)
- sheer fabrics:
    ¼ yard each of two different lace designs
    ¼ yard shimmery gold solid
- ribbon:
    1 yard 2"-wide ivory wire-edge satin ribbon
    6¾ yards ⅜"-wide ivory ribbon
- 2⅛ yards 4"-wide lace trim with scalloped edge
- ½ yard ¼"-wide elastic
- 7 teardrop pearls
- 14 tiny ivory rosebuds
- 1 large ivory rosebud

Pieces to Cut:

- gold shimmery sheer - 7 pieces 3" x 12"
- lace - 4 pieces of each lace design 3" x 12" (total 8 pieces)

How to Make It:

1. Lay the 3" x 12" pieces out, placing one plain gold strip between each of the two alternating laces. Seam them together in one piece. Edgestitch a piece of ⅜" ribbon over each seamline on the right side. Overcast or staystitch all outer edges.

2. Cut a 9" piece of the 4"-wide scalloped lace trim. With right sides together, fold it in half. With the scalloped edge pointing down, fold the top piece open so the scalloped edge is even with the halfway fold underneath. Press flat. Fold both raw ends to the back, creating a square. Press flat. Turn the lace square over and open the pleat. Refold it so it makes a triangular box pleat that is even on both sides. Baste the pleat and folded edges flat. Make a total of seven pleated lace squares.

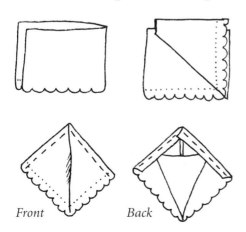

Front   *Back*

3. Beginning at one end of the shade cover, position a pleated lace square over the first seam. Holding it in a diamond position, adjust it so the scalloped edge is directed downward. The left and right corners should just touch the seamlines on the left and right. Baste it flat in place. Repeat across the entire shade cover, creating a deep zigzag hemline.

4. Edgestitch the ⅜" ribbon over the top of the lace squares. Miter the ribbon at each ribbon-trimmed seam.

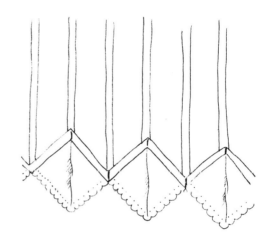

5. With right sides together, stitch the shade cover in a cylinder shape. Topstitch ribbon over this seam and tuck under ¼" at the bottom to finish.

6. Pin the remaining lace trim to the right side around the top edge of the shade cover. Place the straight edge ¾" down from the top edge. Turn under ¼" and butt the ends together. Topstitch it with two rows, spaced ½" apart, to make a casing. Insert the elastic in the casing, adjust it to fit your shade and secure the ends together.

7. Attach a wire-edge ribbon bow to the casing at the top of the shade cover. Hand stitch the large rosebud to the knot of the bow. Tack one small rosebud to each miter point in the ribbon around the bottom. Stitch a teardrop pearl at each space between the lace squares.

COLLECTORS' FANTASY DOLL

Finished Size: 19" tall

WHAT YOU'LL NEED:

Doll Body:
- ½ yard pink moiré
- 1 yard 6"-wide burgundy fringe
- 2 buttons for eyes ⅜" size
- black and red fabric paint
- tiny paint brush
- red embroidery floss
- pink and blue chalk
- large bag stuffing
- 6" length of 1" diameter wooden dowel
- white glue

Doll Dress:
- ¼ yard fuchsia lace
- ½ yard gold sheer
- ½ yard fold lamé
- ⅛ yard purple satin
- 1 yard ¾"-wide woven ribbon
- 3 yards ⅝"-wide gold edge trim
- 1¼ yards ⅛" burgundy/gold twisted cord
- gold metallic thread
- 3 snaps
- 2 gold beads with ⅛" holes

PIECES TO CUT:
FIND THE PATTERNS IN THE PULL-OUT INSERT

Doll:
- pink moiré - cut 1 Doll Chin #42, 1 Doll Head #43: 2 Doll Face #44, 1 Doll Body Front #45, 1 Doll Body Back #46, 1 Doll Sole #47; 4 Doll Arm #48, 4 Doll Leg #49

Doll Dress:
- fuchsia lace - 5 skirt strips 3" x 12"
- gold sheer - 2 Doll Dress Sleeve #52, 5 skirt strips 3" x 12"
- gold lamé - 1 slip 11" x 24"
- purple satin - 1 Doll Dress Bodice Front #50, 2 Doll Dress Bodice Back #51

Shirley Suggests

For easier handling and smoother doll surfaces, fuse lightweight interfacing to the wrong side of your fabric before you cut it out.

HOW TO MAKE IT:

Doll:

1. Stitch all the doll seams using a tiny straight stitch. Make a double row of stitches next to each other and trim the seam allowances to ⅛". With right sides together, sew the Doll Face #44 pieces together at the center. Make the darts in Doll Head #43. Stitch Doll Chin #42 to the head, matching the dots. Sew the face to the chin, matching dots. Turn right side out through the neck.

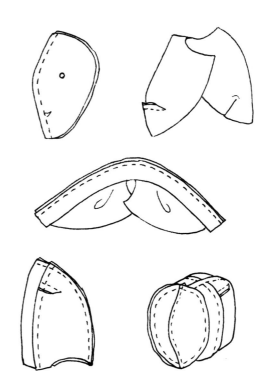

2. With right sides together, stitch two arms, leaving the straight ends open. Leave a 3" opening on the inner arm edge between the dots to stuff the arm.

3. With right sides together, stitch the leg side seams. Leave the straight top edge and foot edge open. With right sides together, stitch the sole to each leg at the foot opening, matching dots to the seams.

4. Fold the open edges of the arms and legs together so the seams are in the center and baste closed.

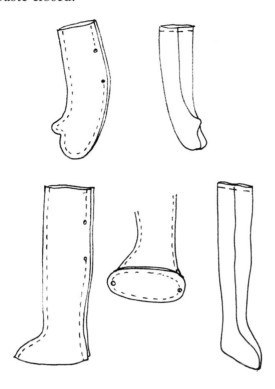

5. With right sides together, stitch the center seam of the body fronts. Baste the arms between the dots at each side, positioning them so the thumbs are directed towards the body. Baste the legs to the lower body between the dots, positioning the toes towards the body.

6. Make the darts in the body backs. With right sides together, stitch the shoulder seams.

7. Place the head inside the body with right sides together. Position the face at the front of the body, match and stitch the neck seam.

8. Stitch the body back center seam together, leaving it open above the dot.

9. Stitch the body front and back together. Be careful to keep the hands, feet, and head from getting caught in the stitching.

10. Turn right side out through the back opening. Stuff the head and the lower half of the body. Insert the wooden dowel into the head, neck, and body. Finish stuffing and slipstitch the center back seam. Stuff the arms and legs to within 1" of the body to allow movement. Slipstitch the openings closed.

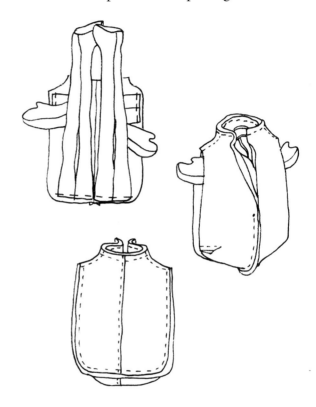

11. Sew the button eyes in place, pulling the thread to the back of the head so they are indented slightly on the face. With red embroidery floss, take a ⅜" stitch at the mouth that crosses the face seam. Pull it to the back of the head and secure so the mouth is indented slightly. Paint the doll's mouth red. Outline the mouth and add five or six eyelashes behind the buttons. Make rosy cheeks with the pink chalk and add a touch of blue eye shadow over the buttons.

12. Cut off about eight 2" lengths of fringe and glue them to the top of the head to form bangs. Glue fringe around the hairline, over the raw ends of the bangs. Fill in the back of the head with rows of the remaining fringe.

Doll Dress:

13. Seam the 3"-wide strips into one piece, alternating the lace and sheer fabrics to make a skirt. Center one purple satin square, on point, at the bottom of each seam, creating a row of purple diamonds at the skirt hemline. Baste the diamonds to the lace and trim away the excess lace and sheer fabric to make a zigzag hemline.

> *Shirley Suggests*
>
> *When working with sheer fabrics, baste tear-away stabilizer to the wrong side. This makes handling easier and allows you to do decorative stitching without any tension problems.*

14. Using metallic thread, machine satin stitch all the skirt seams. Satin stitch the top edge of the purple diamonds. Baste the gold trim to the bottom edge of the purple diamonds and then satin stitch them in place. Stitch the center back seam of the skirt, leaving 3" open at the top edge.

15. With right sides together, stitch the bodice shoulder seams. Gather the top and bottom edges of each sleeve. Also make a row of gathers on the line to make a double puffed sleeve. Insert the sleeves into the bodice armholes. Stitch the side seams and sleeve seams, leaving 1" open at the wrist edges. Topstitch a 5½" length of ribbon as a cuff at each wrist edge. Add gold trim and satin stitch both sides of the ribbon. Turn in the ends to finish and add a snap for a wrist closure.

16. Gather the top edge of the skirt and stitch it to the bodice waistline. Seam the lamé into a slip as you did for the skirt. Hem the lower edge and gather the waistline. Baste it to the bodice waistline.

17. Clip the neckline edge and press under ¼". Topstitch the gold trim around the neckline. Cut two 9" pieces of ribbon for the collar. Hem the front ends of each piece. Gather 4" of each piece to make the back neckline. Couch 18" of cord to the gathered neckline edge of each ribbon piece. Baste the raw ends of the collar pieces to the center back bodice. Turn under ¼", topstitch, and sew a snap at the neckline. Tie the ends of the cord at the front. Add beads to the ends of the cord and knot.

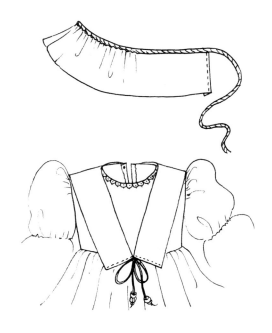

> *Shirley Suggests*
>
> *To finish the doll, add a large bow and a ribbon lily from Chapter Four to the hair.*

Chapter Ten

UPSTAIRS ACCESSORIES

limbing the stairs, your peripheral vision catches a repeated image carved in each step. Elaborate brackets with seemingly no purpose entertain your view as you ascend. This engaging little shape begged for a spot in these pages as well as a more meaningful use. Putting something beautiful to work has provided me with the best of both worlds.

Fancy and Functional

The elegant curved lines of the carving presented a challenge if they were to be more than mere embellishment. The graceful edge shape worked out beautifully as a beaded lampshade and a handy wall pocket. The desk blotter and bookends translate the carved textures almost line by line with the use of stitches and trims.

BEADED LAMPSHADE

Finished Size: 13" high with 44" bottom edge

What You'll Need:

- 13" high square lampshade to embellish
- 1 yard medium blue print
- ½ yard dark blue brocade
- 4½ yards gold braid trim
- ½ yard 3"-wide gold crinkled ribbon
- ½ yard heavy fusible interfacing
- 4 brass bow charms
- purple metallic thread
- beads:

Note: Each side of the shade has about 32 beaded fringe strands. Adjust to fit your shade and calculate the number of beads needed.

    192 small lavender rocaille or seed beads
    256 medium round purple beads
    256 dark blue bugle beads
    128 large round purple beads
    128 gold bugle beads
    128 gold seed beads
    128 gold medium round beads
- beading thread, needle, and beading board

Pieces to Cut:
Find the pattern in the pull-out insert

- blue print fabric - trace one side (¼) of the lampshade on pattern paper and add ¾" to all sides; cut 4
- dark blue brocade fabric - hold Beaded Lampshade #53 on the side of your shade. The finished (no seam allowance) corners of the pattern piece should touch the corners of the shade. Adjust the pattern to fit your shade if necessary; cut 4
- gold crinkle ribbon - trace the oval from Beaded Lampshade #53; add ¼" all around; cut 4
- fusible interfacing - using the dark blue brocade panels as patterns, cut 4 and trim off the seam allowances

---

Shirley Suggests

To make the beading much easier, finish and bead each panel before gluing it to the lampshade covered in the coordinating blue print.

How to Make It:

1. Fuse the interfacing to the wrong side of each panel. Press the fabric seam allowances over the interfacing to the wrong side.

2. Cut out the oval-shaped window. Using metallic thread, satin stitch around the oval window. Topstitch the gold braid next to the satin stitching, butting the ends at the center bottom point. Glue a bow charm over the ends of the braid.

3. Couch the gold braid to the edge on all three sides of the panel. Use a narrow zigzag stitch, butting and finishing the ends at one corner. Satin stitch with metallic thread next to the braid trim.

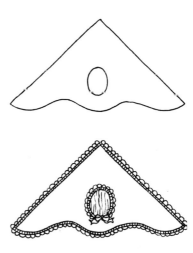

4. Using the braid on the lower curved edge as a spacer, make one strand of beaded fringe spaced ½" apart. Place the beads in the following order on the beading board:

    1 gold medium round
    6 lavender seed beads
    1 gold bugle bead
    1 medium round purple
    1 dark blue bugle
    1 large round purple
    1 dark blue bugle
    1 medium round purple
    1 gold seed bead
    (this bead is the stop)

5. Using beading thread, take a small stitch through the gold braid. Insert your needle through the beads. Skipping the gold seed bead at the end, put the needle back through all the beads. Secure it to the gold braid with a knot and a dot of glue. Take a ½" stitch on the back side of the braid to the next spot and repeat to make another strand of fringe. Cover the entire curved edge of each panel with beaded fringe.

6. Apply a thin coat of glue to the base shade and cover it with blue print fabric. Turn under the fabric raw edges at the corners, top, and bottom and glue them in place. Position the beaded panels around the shade so the corners meet and the fringe extends below the base shade. Glue them in place.

Shirley Suggests

To make the beading go faster, lay several strands of beads out on the beading board ahead of time so you can pick them up in order simply by sliding your needle through them.

DESK BLOTTER

Finished Size: 16" x 20" (or size to fit your desk)

WHAT YOU'LL NEED:

- ½ yard green textured faux suede
- 4⅛ yards ⅛"-wide antique gold cord
- ½ yard 3"-wide gold mesh ribbon
- ¼ yard heavy fusible interfacing
- felt the size of the blotter
- 4 gold half-round brass studs
- gold metallic thread
- heavy cardboard and decorative blotter paper in your size

PIECES TO CUT:
FIND THE PATTERN IN THE PULL-OUT INSERT

- green suede - 8 Blotter Corner #54
- interfacing - 4 Blotter Corner #54

HOW TO MAKE IT:

1. Fuse the interfacing to the wrong side of four suede corners. Transfer the spiral design and triangle appliqué to the right side of the fabric. With right sides together, stitch the curved edge of one interfaced corner to one plain corner. Trim, turn, and press.

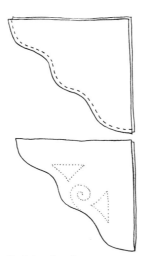

2. Couch the cord to the finished edge, beginning at one straight side and tucking the end to the wrong side where the spiral begins. Working from the other direction, couch the cord in the same way, crossing on to the fabric at the beginning of the spiral. Cut it off, leaving an 8" end. Curl the end of the cord to match the design and couch it down. Trim the end off neatly in the center and cover with a brass stud.

3. Trace the triangular appliqué pattern on paper and cut eight from the mesh ribbon. Baste two in place on the corner and satin stitch them down with gold metallic thread. Repeat to make a total of four corners.

4. Cut the cardboard and blotter paper to the size desired. Position the corners in place. Fold the extra fabric to the back side. Glue it in place, mitering corners for a flat finish. Glue the felt to the back side to cover the raw edges.

Shirley Suggests

Use this same design to make bookends. Simply make two corners as for the blotter. Glue them to a set of purchased metal bookends or have wooden shapes cut to match and cover them with matching fabric.

Project

WISHES WALL POCKET

Finished Size: 10" x 14" high

WHAT YOU'LL NEED:

- ½ yard gold moiré
- ½ yard fleece
- ½ yard 4"-wide gold fringe
- 2½ yards 1¼"-wide ivory woven ribbon
- 2 yards ⅛" ivory/gold twisted cord
- brass label frame
- heavy flexible cardboard
- white glue

PIECES TO CUT:
FIND THE PATTERNS IN THE PULL-OUT INSERT

- gold moiré - 1 Wall Pocket Front #55,
  2 Wall Pocket Back #56
- cardboard - 1 Wall Pocket Front #55,
  1 Wall Pocket Back #56, eliminating seam allowances
- fleece - 1 Wall Pocket Front #55,
  1 Wall Pocket Back #56 using the cardboard as a pattern

HOW TO MAKE IT:

1. Glue the fleece to the corresponding cardboard pieces. With the right side out, pin the moiré to the fleece on each piece. Allow the fabric to extend over the edge evenly on all sides. Fold the fabric to the back side and glue flat, mitering the corners neatly. On the back section, glue the second piece of moiré to cover the raw edges. Use sharp scissors to trim off the seam allowance around the entire outer edge.

2. Glue the fringe to the back section along the bottom straight edges.

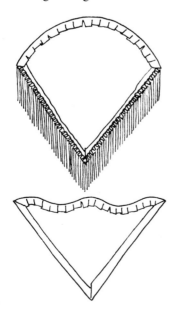

3. Gently curve the front section so it bows slightly. Glue it to the back over the fringe.

4. Glue the cording around the entire front section, ending at one upper corner. Glue cording across the curved upper edge of the back section.

5. Cut a 32" piece of ribbon for a handle. Make sure it's not twisted and glue the ends to the back at the upper corners.

6. Cut the remaining ribbon in half. Tie two bows and glue one to each upper corner on the front section.

7. Make a label and glue it to the inside of the frame on the front about ½" down from the top edge. Bend the frame slightly as needed to fit the front section.

Chapter Eleven

Making an Entrance

*A*s you take your first step across the threshold, there is little tendency to look down. Covered with grime when I first saw it, the tiles dared me to be distracted. This foyer floor makes a dramatic bid for your attention with more than one surprise in store. Patchwork tiles in unexpected color combinations remind you of an old quilt. Looking closer, they reveal a stenciled design that dropped me to my knees when I discovered it.

Stenciled Mosaic

This stenciled tile design offers endless possibilities for appliqué, quilting, and embroidery uses. The footstool, quilt, and frames demonstrate the versatility of this elegant pattern when it is used in dramatically different sizes. It works equally well with or without the patchwork tile background.

 # FANCY FOOTSTOOL

Finished Size: 14" x 14" x 8" high

What You'll Need:

- footstool to cover

Note: Measure your footstool and adjust yardages as needed.

- 2 yards plaid fabric
- ½ yard burgundy brocade fabric
- ½ yard paper-backed appliqué fusible
- ¾ yard fleece
- copper metallic thread
- 4 purple cord drapery tie-backs with tassels
- 1" cover button

Pieces to Cut:
Find the patterns in the pull-out insert

- plaid fabric and fleece - measure the top of the footstool and add 6" to all sides, cut 1, centering the plaid design
- appliqué fusible - trace the footstool appliqué pieces to the paper side and roughly cut out the square
- burgundy brocade - fuse the appliqué pieces to the wrong side and cut out on the lines, following the manufacturer's instructions

Shirley Suggests

This is a slipcover for a footstool. This makes it easy to remove for cleaning or a change of look. This design will also make a terrific appliquéd pillow front if you aren't a footstool fan.

How to Make It:

1. Using Footstool Appliqué #57 as a placement guide, remove the paper and fuse the brocade to the right side of the plaid.

2. Baste the fleece to the wrong side. Satin stitch the raw edges of the appliqué design with metallic thread.

3. Cover the button with brocade and stitch it down to the center of the appliqué.

4. Working over the footstool with the wrong side out, fold the fabric down over the sides and dart them to fit at each corner. Remove the cover and stitch the darts. Trim the excess fabric.

5. With the top in place, measure the length for the skirt and add 3". Measure the perimeter of the footstool and add 16" for box pleats at each corner. Cut a piece of plaid to these measurements. Stitch the skirt in a ring. Fold it in quarters beginning with the seam and mark with pins. Pin the skirt to the top with right sides together. Match the quarter marks to each corner. Make an inverted box pleat at each corner, using up all the excess fabric. Stitch the skirt to the top.

6. Press crease lines at the pleats. Mark the skirt hem length, press it up, and stitch on the wrong side.

7. With the cover in place on the footstool, wrap the tie-backs around the skirt seamline. Knot them together at each corner over the pleats. Hand tack the cord and knots in place.

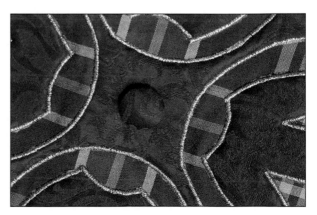

FOREVER FRAMES

Finished Size: 9" x 9" square with 4" x 4" photo opening;
11" x 13" rectangle with 5" x 7" photo opening

WHAT YOU'LL NEED:

(to make one frame)
- ¼ yard ivory moiré
- ¼ yard fleece
- 2½ yards ⅛" ivory/gold twisted cord
- antique gold fabric stencil paints
- plastic stencil material
- small stencil brush
- small utility knife
- ⅜"-thick foam core
- white glue

PIECES TO CUT:
FIND THE PATTERNS IN THE PULL-OUT INSERT

- ivory moiré - 4 frames pieces #58 or #59 and #60

HOW TO MAKE IT:

1. Trace one stencil design on stencil material and cut it out with a utility knife.

2. Using the frame pattern as a placement guide, stencil the gold design on the ivory moiré pieces. Allow them to dry thoroughly.

3. Seam the frame pieces together. Note that the small frame has mitered corners. Leave the seams open at the dots.

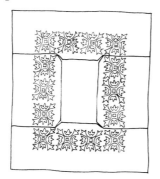

4. Cut the foam core base for the frame as follows: small - 9" x 9" frame back and a front with centered 4" x 4" opening; large - 11" x 13" frame back and a front with a centered 5" x 7" opening; easel - 3" x 7".

5. Glue the fleece to the frame base and trim off the excess even with the foam core edges. Pin the stenciled front to the fleece. Fold the excess fabric to the back of the frame.

6. Glue a piece of ivory moiré to the back and trim it even with the frame edges.

7. Glue the cording to the frame edges. The small frame has cord on the mitered seamlines.

8. Cover both sides of the frame back as you did before. Cover the easel in the same way.

9. Glue the back to the wrong side of the frame front, leaving one side open to insert photos. Using a 3" long piece of fabric as a hinge, glue the easel to the back. Place it so the frame will stand up. Using a 3" length of cord, make a "stay" that attaches the base of the frame to the bottom of the easel. Glue securely.

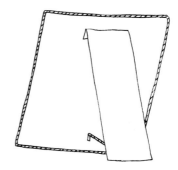

SATIN PARLOR QUILT

Finished Size: 80" x 80" plus fringe

WHAT YOU'LL NEED:

- taffeta fabric:
    1 yard each blue and bronze
    3 yards red
- satin fabric:
    1 yard purple
    1 yard ivory
    2 yards tan
- 9 yards 4"-wide gold fringe
- 5 yards black cotton quilt backing
- cotton quilt batting
- antique gold fabric stencil paints
- plastic stencil material
- small stencil brush
- small utility knife

PIECES TO CUT:
FIND THE PATTERNS IN THE PULL-OUT INSERT

- red taffeta - 17 blocks 5½" x 5½"; 6"-wide borders to equal 10 yards
- blue taffeta - 160 Parlor Quilt #62; 2"-wide borders to equal 10 yards
- bronze taffeta - 12 blocks 5½" x 5½"
- purple satin - 24 blocks 5½" x 5½"
- ivory satin - 160 Parlor Quilt #62; 3"-wide borders to equal 10 yards
- tan satin - 244 Parlor Quilt #63

HOW TO MAKE IT:

1. Using Parlor Quilt Stencil #61 as a guide, trace the design on the stencil material and cut it out. Stencil the fabric blocks as follows:
    red taffeta - 17 blocks
    purple satin - 24 blocks
    bronze taffeta - 12 blocks

2. Make 80 of Unit A.

Unit A

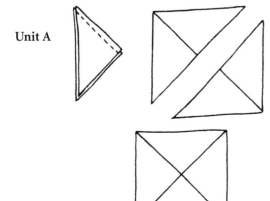

3. Make 53 of Unit B as follows:
    red - 17 blocks
    bronze - 12 blocks
    purple - 24 blocks

Unit B

4. Assemble four main patchwork sections, following the quilt layout.

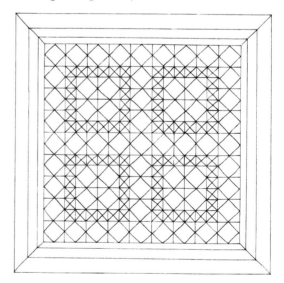

5. Add top, middle, and bottom borders to form two vertical sections.

6. Add three vertical borders of Unit B blocks to finish the quilt top.

7. Stitch the borders to the quilt top in the following order:
>blue - 2"-wide
>ivory - 3"-wide
>red - 6"-wide

8. Cut the quilt backing in two equal pieces. Seam them together. Working flat, layer the backing, batting, and patchwork quilt top. Trim all the raw edges evenly and baste them together. Thoroughly baste the layers of the quilt together before picking it up. Don't use safety pins as they will make large holes in the fabrics and leave marks that you may not be able to remove.

9. Hand or machine quilt in the ditch of the patchwork and border seamlines.

Shirley Suggests

This is a large quilt to stitch, so you may want to tie it at the patchwork intersections using gold embroidery floss. This saves a lot of time without changing the look of the quilt.

10. Remove the basting from the edge of the quilt. Stitch the fringe to the quilt top and batting layers. Looking from the back side, fold under the raw edge of the backing fabric and hand stitch it to the back of the fringe.

About the Author

Shirley Botsford has always seen things through the eye of a needle. Having made her first quilt at the age of four, she's been involved in every aspect of sewing and needle arts for the last 25 years. Working as a professional in the home decorating, fashion, sewing, and craft fields, Shirley feels her real specialty is teaching. The author of *Daddy's Ties*, she lectures, give workshops at quilt events across the country, and holds retreats for stitchers at Botsford Briar, her 1889 Queen Anne Victorian. Nicknamed "The Stitch Inn," it has provided the inspiration for the projects showcased in the pages of this book.

Her popular ready-to-wear ensembles have been seen in the Fairfield Fashion Show for ten years. Look for her award-winning designs with Simplicity Patterns, articles for *Threads* magazine, and monthly bylines, "The Village Stitchsmith" and "The Designer's Hope Chest," featured in *Country Decorating Ideas* and *Country Almanac*.

Claire Shaeffer's Fabric Sewing Guide. Krause Publications, 1994

Complete Guide to Sewing. Reader's Digest Association, 1976 revised version

Complete Guide to Needlework. Reader's Digest Association, 1979

Creating Texture with Textiles by Linda McGehee. Krause Publications, 1998

Shirley Botsford's Daddy's Ties, Krause Publications, 1994

The Art of Manipulating Fabric by Collette Wolff, Krause Publications, 1996

The Complete Book of Machine Embroidery by Robbie and Tony Fanning, Krause Publications, 1986

The Complete Book of Machine Quilting by Robbie and Tony Fanning, Krause Publications, 1994

Sources

Batting, Stuffing, Pillow Forms and Pellets
Fairfield Processing Corp.
88 Rose Hill Ave.
PO Box 1157
Danbury, CT 06813

Beads
TWE Beads
PO Box 55
Hamburg, NJ 07419

Boxes to Cover
Calico Moon Handcrafts
1919 State St.
Salem, OR 97301

Braiding Supplies
Craft House International
328 North Westwood Ave.
Toledo, OH 43607-3343

Buttons
JHB International, Inc.
1955 South Quince St.
Denver, CO 80231

Charms
Decorative Charms and Brass Label Frames
Creative Beginnings
475 Morro Bay
Morro Bay, CA 93442

Embroidery Ribbon
Bucilla
1 Oak Ridge Rd.
Hazelton, PA 18201

Fabric
Capital Imports
PO Box 13002
Tallahassee, FL 32317
lace

Hi-Fashion Fabrics
483 Broadway
New York, NY 10013
specialty cottons

J.B. Martin Co., Inc.
10 East 53rd St.
New York, NY 10022
velvet

Marcus Brothers Textiles, Inc.
1460 Broadway
New York, NY 10036
quilter's flannel

Rosebar Textiles
93 Entin Road
Clifton, NJ 07014
taffeta, moiré and satin

Springs Industries
PO Box 10232
Rock Hill, SC 29731
muslin and cottons

Framing Boards and Supplies
Pres-On Merchandising Corp.
1020 South Westgate
Addison, IL 60101

Fusibles
Freundenberg Pellon Corp.
3440 Eno Industrial Dr.
Durham, NC 27704

Heat 'n Bond
Therm O Web Inc.
770 Glen Ave.
Wheeling, IL 60090

Glue
Tacky Glue
Aleene's, Div. of Artis, Inc.
85 Industrial Way
Buellton, CA 93427

Interfacing
Freundenberg Pellon Corp.
3440 Eno Industrial Dr.
Durham, NC 27704

Needlework Fabric
Kraeinik Manufacturing Co., Inc.
3106 Timanus La, Suite 101
Baltimore, MD 21244

Ribbon
Elsie's Exquisites
PO Box 7177
Laguna Niguel, CA 92607

Offray Ribbon Co.
360 Rt. 24
Chester, NJ 07930

Sewing Machines
Bernina of America, Inc.
3500 Thayer Ct.
Aurora, IL 60504

Pfaff of America, Inc.
610 Winters Ave.
Paramus, NJ 07653

Viking & White Sewing Machines
11760 Berea Rd.
Cleveland, OH 44111

Stenciling Supplies
Aleene's, Div. of Artis, Inc.
85 Industrial Way
Buellton, CA 93427

Thread
Coats & Clark, Inc.
Two Lakepointe Plaza
4145 South Stream Blvd.
Charlotte, NC 28217

Sulky of America
3113 Broadpoint Dr.
Harbor Heights, FL 33983

Web of Threads
3240 Lone Oak Rd., Suite 124
Paducah, KY 42003

Tools
Clothilde, Inc.
2200 South Ocean Ln., #802
Fort Lauderdale, FL 33316
The Perfect Pleater and sewing accessories

Olfa Products, Div. of General Housewares Corp.
1536 Beech St.
Terre Haute, IN 47803
rotary cutters and accessories

Omnigrid
1560 Port Dr.
Burlington, WA 98233
rulers and rotary cutting mats

Prym-Dritz Corp.
PO Box 5038
Spartanburg, SC 29304
Fray Check and sewing accessories

Trims
Conso Products Co.
PO Box 326
513 N. Duncan By-Pass
Union, SC 29349

Wm. E. Wrights/Boye
85 South St.
W. Warren, MA 01092

Wood Products
Walnut Hollow Farm
1409 State Rd. 23
Dodgeville, WI 53533
folding screens and boxes

Create Beautiful Decor for Your Home

The Secrets of Fashioning Ribbon Flowers
Heirlooms For the Next Generation
by Helen Gibb

What to do with all that gorgeous ribbon available today? Easy, fashion the most elegant flowers imaginable. Incorporate 15 different flowers into jewelry, home decor, wearables, and more. Included are instructions for making the leaves, calyx, and stems.

Softcover • 8¼ x 10⅞ • 128 pages • 150 b&w Illustrations • 100 color photos
FFFGD • $24.95

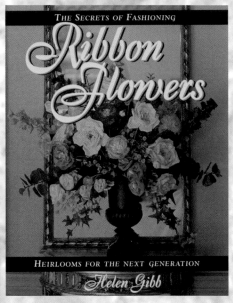

Shirley Botsford's Daddy's Ties
by Shirley Botsford

Shirley Botsford unknots some creative ideas for Dad's old, unused ties. Learn to make great keepsakes and one-of-a-kind gifts. Complete patterns, step-by-step instructions, and full-color illustrations show you how to make quilts, picture frames, and dozens of other beautiful treasures.

Softcover • 8¼ x 10⅞ • 128 pages color throughout
DADTI • $21.50

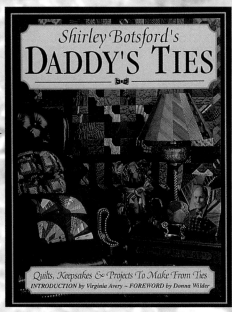

Fabulous Floorcloths
Create Contemporary Floor Coverings from an Old World Art
by Caroline O'Neill Kuchinsky

The first book dedicated to making canvas floorcloths. Contemporary or antique, a floorcloth transforms an ordinary floor into a work of art. The step-by-step instructions guide you through projects easily. Choose designs and color schemes in 14 projects divided into simple to advanced.

Softcover • 8¼ x 10⅞ • 128 pages • 60 color photos • 225 color diagrams
FLODEC • $19.95

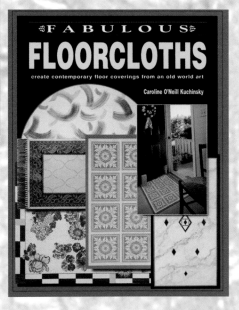

Call to receive a **FREE** catalog of our complete product line.

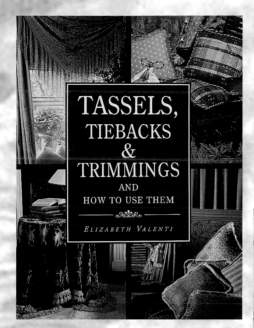
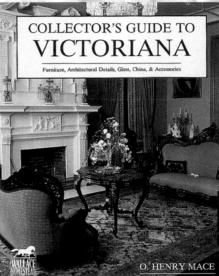
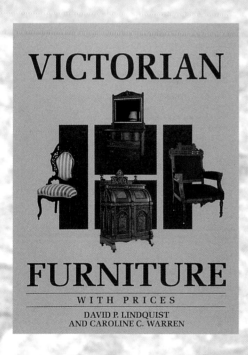